THE BACK HOME SERIES

Carolyn Schroeder, Easter Sunday, April 18, 1954
North Freedom, Wisconsin

Praise for
Carolyn Dallmann

Carolyn Dallmann captures the innocence of a little girl growing up on a farm in a small rural Wisconsin community. Through lessons learned, the love of family, the joys of a close-knit neighborhood, and the real-life challenges of operating a farm, the author offers a charming glimpse of rural Midwestern life in the 1950s and 1960s where a party telephone line was the definition of social media. A gentle read that is sure to entertain.

—Keri Olson, author of *Find Your Heart, Follow Your Heart*

North Freedom, by Carolyn Dallmann, has a wonderful immediacy, a rawness. The prose is not the work of a professional author, but that of a talented amateur venturing into deep waters for the first time; this seems a strength, a meeting of form and function, giving this memoir a sense of rustic authority that might otherwise be lacking—almost as if it were written in a sort of Wisconsin dialect. The result is a text with the rural authenticity of a Grandma Moses painting. *North Freedom* is reminiscent of August Derleth's *Walden West*, but sweeter—imagine Derleth with the addition of a generous dose of Laura Ingalls Wilder's *Little House in the Big Woods*. The rural charm and humor of these reminiscences is delightful. Wonderful family photos add to this portrait of mid-20th-century rural Wisconsin.

—Marc Seals, University of Wisconsin-Platteville
Baraboo Sauk County

This book is a gem and a joy to read! Growing up in North Freedom, it was delightful to reminisce as well as to learn more about the history of my hometown. Every page brought back pleasant memories of bygone days; days to treasure in my heart.

—Carolyn (Myers) Blum, author of *Dedicated*

Series Titles

North Freedom
Carolyn Dallmann

Ohio Apertures
Robert Miltner

North Freedom

a memoir

Carolyn Dallmann

Cornerstone Press
Stevens Point, Wisconsin

Cornerstone Press, Stevens Point, Wisconsin 54481
Copyright © 2022 Carolyn Dallmann
www.uwsp.edu/cornerstone

Printed in the United States of America by
Point Print and Design Studio, Stevens Point, Wisconsin 54481

Library of Congress Control Number: 2021949397
ISBN: 978-1-7377390-2-9

All rights reserved.

This is a work of creative nonfiction. All of the events in this book are true to the best of the author's memory and research. The author in no way represents any company, corporation, or brand, mentioned herein. The views expressed in this memoir are solely those of the author. This book or any portion thereof may not be reproduced or used in any manner whatsoever without the express written permission of the author except for the use of a brief quotation in a book review.

Cornerstone Press titles are produced in courses and internships offered by the Department of English at the University of Wisconsin–Stevens Point.

Director & Publisher	Executive Editor	Senior Editors
Dr. Ross K. Tangedal	Jeff Snowbarger	Lexie Neeley & Monica Swinick

Senior Editorial Assistant
Gavrielle McClung

Press Staff
Megan Bittner, Kala Buttke, Grace Dahl, Camilla Freund, Kyra Goedken, Amanda Green, Brett Hill, Seth Kundinger, Amanda Leibham, Dylan Potter, Cassie Ress, Annika Rice, Abbi Rohde, Bethany Webb

*To Harold and Pearl (Kaun) Schroeder, with love.
And for Cooper Erich Herbes and Zoe Harper Herbes.*

The Schroeder Family, Easter Sunday, March 29, 1959
Harold and Pearl (Kaun) Schroeder
David, Randy, Allen, and Carolyn

Contents

Preface	xi
The Half Mile Road	1
The Upper Farm	27
The Lower Farm	99
Crops	123
Animals	185
The Forty	223
Church	237
Neighbors	273
Visits	291
North Freedom Grade School	315
Acknowledgments	337
Bibliography	341
Notes	343

Preface

As a baby boomer (born 1947), I frequently recall memories of my childhood. I grew up on a farm in the small village of North Freedom, Wisconsin, in the 1950s and 60s. My three brothers (David, 1948; Allen, 1949; Randy, 1956) and I often reminisce about that bygone era, with each of us recalling events from our unique perspectives. We shared stories about our relatives, people from the village and life on the farm. As I repeated these stories to my grandchildren, they said, "Grandma, I wish we could do those things, but our lives are different." Thus, I wrote this book to preserve the way of life I enjoyed as a child during that seemingly innocent time. Life today *is* different than it was seven decades ago.

The stories and dialogue in the book are supported by facts found in published documents and papers about the village. These documents and family records confirmed our recollections of dates and the people. Brothers David and Randy continued to live in the village as adults and remembered valuable details about farm buildings and equipment. Brother Allen, who lives in Arizona, was exceptionally helpful with researching the families and the land they owned. During more recent conversations with my brothers, forgotten memories were triggered. This enabled the characters in the book to be portrayed dynamically in the roles they played.

The book is organized into ten sections. If they are read consecutively, there will be some redundancy. However, if stories are read individually, some detail may be lost. In *The Half Mile Road*, we are introduced to my grandparents, Hilda and Louis Kaun; my parents, Harold and Pearl Schroeder; and the Schroeder children: Carolyn, David, Allen, and Randy. *The Upper Farm* describes our family's land, which included two adjacent farms known as the "upper farm" and the "lower farm." The upper farm is the home where I grew up. Also included in this section is a look at the "uptown" area of North Freedom; the business part of the village was three or four blocks west of our home, where Maple and Oak Streets intersect Walnut Street. *The Lower Farm* introduces the home of Hilda and Louis Kaun, who lived there in 1948 when my parents and I moved to the village, and where most of the farm operations took place.

Crops and *Animals* detail the life of our farm, from raising corn and oats to cows and pigs, while *The Forty* recounts anecdotes of activities and events that occurred on the 40 acres of pasture and woodland that our family owned in the bluffs near North Freedom. *Church* tells about unique experiences that happened in our small church building, and *Neighbors* illustrates the folks who lived on East Walnut Street, close to the upper farm. *Visits* describes the short trips our family took, a necessity given that long vacations were not possible due to the day-to-day demands of a working farm, and *North Freedom Grade School* closes the story with recollections of school activities and experiences, ending with my eighth grade graduation.

* * *

Candid photographs of some of the prominent people from my childhood were not found. These people are shown on the following pages, in more formal settings. Although these photographs are from a time that is different than that covered in the book, the pictures closely represent my memories of the people.

Louis and Hilda (Beckman) Kaun
September 24, 1966

The Schroeder brothers, their occupations, and their spouses:

Harold—Farmer, married Pearl Kaun (Carolyn's parents)
Richard—Farmer, married Margaret Schuldt
Herman—Farmer, married Idella Thorsen
Louis "Turk"—Shoe store owner, married Elsie Klinskie
Walter—Baker (worked for Hugo), married Louise Ellenez
Martin—Farmer, married Martha Kohlmeyer
Rudolph—Farmer, married Edna Meyer
Hugo—Bakery owner, married Julia Sylling
Paul—Grader operator for the county, married Amy Anderson
Elmer—Farmer, married Ada Dierson
Albert "Doc"—Farmhand, never married

Harold Schroeder (my father) and his brothers, 1920.

Front row: Harold, Richard
Middle row: Herman, Louis "Turk", Walter, Martin, Rudolph
Back row: Hugo, Paul, Elmer, Albert "Doc"

Hilda (Beckman) Kaun's family, circa 1920.
Front row: Martha (Beckman) Janzen, Ida M. (Dieckman), August Ferdinand Beckman, Emma Beckman
Back row: Hilda (Beckman) Kaun (maternal grandmother), Rudolph "Rudy," John, Alma (Beckman) Tewes (Hilda's stepbrothers and stepsister)

* * *

Dad's father, Herman Schroeder, my grandpa, died when Dad was five years old. He was born in Hanover, Germany and immigrated to the United States. Grandpa Schroeder was married twice. He and his first wife, Ida Wegener, had seven sons, then they had a baby girl, Luella.

Their youngest son, Elmer, had just turned two years old before Luella was born on April 26, 1907. Sadly, Ida died on May 11, 1907. Luella died on May 20, 1907.

Following these tragic events, Grandpa Schroeder's older brother, Heinrich and his wife Martha, known as Hank and Meta, approached Grandpa Schroeder. They were concerned that little Elmer required more attention than Grandpa and the other six boys could provide. Walter, the oldest of the other six brothers, was only 11 when his mother died. Hugo, the youngest of the other six, was four years old.

Hank and Meta owned a farm in Eitzen, close to Caledonia. They did not have children of their own. It may be assumed that Hank and Meta stepped in to help Grandpa Schroeder during the nine days between Ida's and Luella's deaths, possibly longer. Grandpa and his sons had to run the farm and the house, while dealing with their grief.

Hank and Meta offered to take Elmer into their home and raise him as if he were their own. Grandpa Schroeder agreed. Over the years the two families spent many happy times together. But Hank and Meta raised Elmer.

Grandpa Schroeder married my Grandma, Wilhelmine "Minnie" (Tewes) Schroeder, on March 20, 1908. They had four sons. Dad was the second youngest. Grandpa died on July 28, 1917.

I had no aunts or uncles on Mom's side of the family. Mom was an only child. Grandma Hilda's father, my great grandfather, had two wives; his first wife passed away. Therefore, Grandma Hilda had older stepbrothers and a stepsister. My maternal great-grandparents are in the middle of the front row.

My great aunts Martha, Emma and Alma were considered my aunts. We saw them several times each month. Rudy was close to our family but lived almost 50 miles away so we did not see him as often. John was involved with his family and we saw even less of him.

My maternal grandfather's family was more fractured. We saw a couple of Grandpa Louie's brothers and a sister once a year or so. Two of Grandpa's brothers lived in Montana.

North Freedom, Wisconsin

1   Bank
2   Baraboo River
3   Canning Factory
4   Depot
5   Dickie's Land
6   Grandma Hilda and Grandpa Louie's House
7   Half Mile Road
8   Horseshoe
9   Lower Farm
10 Lower Pasture
11 North Freedom Grade School
12 Park
13 Post Office
14 Railroad Tracks
15 Schroeder Ponds
16 St. Paul's Lutheran Church
17 Trestle
18 Upper Farm
19 Upper Pasture
20 Uptown
21 Walnut Street

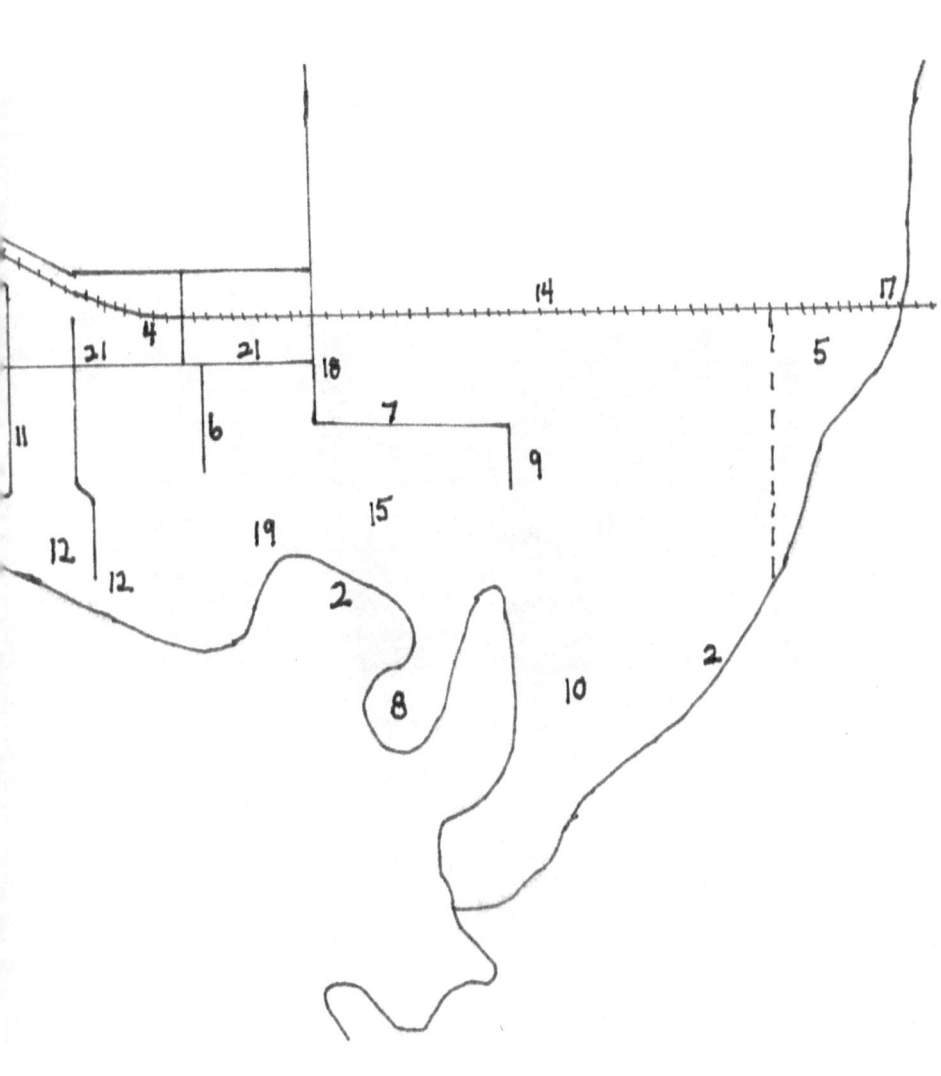

L to R: David, Allen, and Carolyn Schroeder, in the drive between their home on the upper farm and their neighbor's home, several days after the Blizzard of 1959.

The Half Mile Road

1
The Blizzard of 1959

The winter of 1959 was the first time I did not feel safe on the farm. I was 11 years old. It was not the snow and cold that unsettled me. I had experienced that before. What scared me was the way Mom and Dad said this snowstorm was a blizzard. Their planning was done in throaty low tones not meant for my ears: "How will you?—I don't think we can—Pearl—logging sled—drifts—milk cows"—I could hear only snippets of the conversation.

I always felt safe and protected at home because I knew what to expect. This change of activities made me anxious. Then I heard them say Dad would not return home that night. That had never happened before. I did not know when I would see him again. I did not like this ominous blizzard.

Mom packed food into a big pail. Our house on the upper farm became exceptionally quiet as she scurried about the kitchen. Dad and Grandpa walked to the lower farm to milk cows, taking the pail of food with them. Driving in this weather might strand a vehicle and complicate the situation.

The road connecting the upper farm to the lower farm was a half mile long. The upper part belonged to the village and ended at the fencerow that marked off the last field before the turn by the house on the lower place. The lower part of the road belonged to us.

Our house was on the upper farm at the east end of Walnut Street in the village of North Freedom, Wisconsin, population about 600. If you traveled east on Walnut Street, the main street, and missed the left turn going out of town, across the railroad tracks, you drove directly into our driveway. We owned 160 acres. Mom and Dad later bought our neighbor's adjacent field, adding 10 more. We had another 40 acres of combination pasture and woodland south of the village that we called the Forty.

Most work was done on the lower farm where Grandma Hilda and Grandpa Louie Kaun lived when we moved to North Freedom in 1948. They moved from that farmhouse to a lovely home in the village on Franklin Street before I started school. However, Grandpa and Dad continued to manage the farm together after their move.

Dad had been managing the Schroeder family farm in Caledonia, Minnesota, for his mother, my grandma Wilhelmine (Minnie) Schroeder, carrying out a responsibility he had assumed years before. Dad's father, my grandpa Herman Schroeder, died when Dad was five years old. We moved after Grandma Minnie's death and the sale of the Schroeder farm, because Grandpa Louie, Mom's father, was getting older and needed help. This support of aging parents was not unusual where family farms were concerned.

I was fortunate that our farm was located in the village because I was exposed to a social experience many of my classmates missed. Kids living in the countryside were more isolated. They did not see daily activities of neighbors or hear conversations in the post office and grocery stores uptown. Likewise, children living in the village were not exposed to the disciplines of farm life: how machinery used for planting and harvest works, what it takes to maintain a dairy operation, and the many associated intricacies of a family farm. However, the snow, wind and freezing temperatures of the Blizzard of 1959 challenged families living in both the village and the country.

The village maintained their part of the half mile road better than we maintained our part. Ours consisted of two tire tracks with grass in the middle. The village part was the same except they added gravel to some of the tire tracks, especially where the road got mushy during spring thaw. Mom and Dad did not want too much maintenance on our road; it was a means of discouraging people from coming onto our property.

The village did not plow snow off their part of the road until a maintenance man, Phil Zimmerly, was hired. Phil was hired a couple years after we moved to North Freedom. Dad asked the village to have Phil plow the upper part of the road because it belonged to the village.

Phil approached Dad about a problem he ran into. "They told me to plow only the village part. I need to turn the rig around in the middle of the road, but I don't want to tear up your fields. That truck with the plow attached takes a wide swath."

"Well," Dad said. "That is a predicament. Maybe you could use the circle drive around our milk house on the lower farm for your turn. Would that work?"

Phil hesitated knowing he would need to plow our part of the road to the lower farm to get to the circle drive. "I don't know about that. The old ladies uptown might complain."

"I see." Dad knew exactly which ladies Phil was worried about but did not say anything while he waited for Phil to consider his options.

"Maybe we just won't tell anyone that I plowed your part of the road." Dad thought Phil's suggestion was a wonderful idea and assured Phil he would not mention the extra plowing to anyone.

The plan was implemented. The village plow truck did not drive on our fields. The circle drive around our milk house at the lower farm was an efficient means for Phil to make his turn while helping us. And, this explains why the village snowplowing truck got stuck in the corner turn of the road by our lower farm following the Blizzard of 1959. Doubtless, there were raised eyebrows at the time, but the village continued to plow the entire half mile road from that day forward.

Maintenance of the road, or lack thereof, was abundantly clear when heavy blowing snow started to accumulate. Dairy operations were conducted in the large barn at the lower place. Milk was collected and stored in 10-gallon cans which were placed in a cooling tank in the milk house. The milk was collected daily by a truck operated by the dairy cooperative out of Reedsburg.

Problems occurred when the milk truck could not negotiate the road to the lower farm. The co-op paid us for the volume of milk we delivered and the measured amount of butterfat it contained. It could be held at or below a specific temperature for three days. After that, it had to be dumped. If the truck could not pick up our milk, there would be no income. During the winter of 1959, the half mile road was snowed in for days. When the snow and wind finally stopped, the temperature dropped drastically.

"What are Dad and Grandpa doing?" The answer to my question likely would increase my anxiety, but I had to ask because the men had not returned.

"They're milking cows." Mom's steady voice was reassuring, but her eyes avoided mine.

Where did they sleep? I wondered but kept the question to myself.

Dad and Grandpa had dressed in their heaviest winter clothes, dragged themselves through drifts, some almost 10 feet tall, to reach the lower farm. Milking cows continued twice daily, but moving the milk to a point where it could be picked up by the co-op was a challenge. All reserve cans were filled. When the cooling tank was full, cans were stashed in snowbanks.

Dad and Grandpa shoveled as the blizzard continued. They planned to use the old wooden logging sled and our two workhorses to pull the milk along the half mile road to Walnut Street. The milk truck from the cooperative could pick it up and haul it from there. The road needed to be shoveled just enough for the horses to get the empty sled through one time. An initial sled track of packed snow would make maneuvering the half mile easier until spring thaw.

It was a challenge for the horses to maneuver through the high white drifts while dragging the empty sled. It would be a bigger challenge for them to pull it loaded with milk over deep snow in subzero temperatures. I watched the daily slow progress of men, horses and sled through drafty panes, half covered with ice crystals, on the south windows of our cozy farmhouse. The huge animals sunk belly deep in snow. Grandpa and Dad were in front of the team shoveling holes for each horse step, strategically choosing a place around (not through) the deepest drifts. I could see their voices in the frosty air as they urged the team forward one step at a time. Their strained mouths were saying words I could not hear, words I should not hear. I had heard those words before. They were not said in the house.

The bodies of the huge animals steamed as they strained and stumbled. Their muzzles dripped strings of drool turning to icicles. Sometimes their front legs bucked high, instinct wanting to avoid the task they needed to perform.

I recalled riding behind the horses on the back of the oats planter with Dad in spring, hearing nothing but the gentle slicing of soil as seeds fell in rows while Dad hummed. The soft clop of giant hooves keeping a rhythm to Dad's tune was a faraway memory. That memory was much different from the straining steaming horses and men I was seeing from my window perch these frosty days.

Mom prepared beef stew, goulash, chicken dumpling soup and sandwiches. She packed it in wide mouth thermos containers and metal lunch buckets. It was midday when she called David, my oldest brother. Her instructions were clear. "Dad and Grandpa need this food. See where they're shoveling?" She pointed to the spot between the swale of the little pasture and the outline of the lower farm that came in and out of view because of the blowing snow. "Cut straight across the field, unless you can't see over a snowdrift. If that happens, go around the drift, but get yourself back on track to the men."

She trusted my brother's uncanny sense of direction. She also knew his instinct to help might be too much to resist. "Do not stay with Dad and Grandpa. Have them point you back to the house. Don't dawdle. The wind is picking up again."

My brother David braved the snow and freezing temperatures to deliver the food to Grandpa and Dad. Only 10 years old, David trudged through or around snowdrifts, some much taller than himself, between the upper farm and to where the men were shoveling.

Watching David head southeast across the field, I asked Mom, "What if he gets lost, and we can't find him?"

"That's not going to happen. David knows the way." Again, Mom's voice was steady, but the dangerous conditions outside tore through me. This was the first of many trips David made carrying food to Dad and Grandpa.

Finally, the first load of milk arrived, only to meet another obstacle where the half mile road met Walnut Street: a huge mountain of snow, frozen solid, created by the village plow. Grandpa damned the village, the plow and anything else that came into his mind. We stayed out of his way when he got like this.

Dad paid Grandpa no mind as he conjured a plan. "Hey there Louie, what do you say we make a slide?"

Grandpa looked away with a "Humph!" Some minutes later Grandpa suggested the perfect spot to initiate this new project which was the exact spot Dad thought would be best.

Compelled to work together, the men struggled to carve a path so they could maneuver heavy, awkward milk cans up the south side of the mountain of snow, teeter and ease them over the top, and slide them down the north side. The cans were then encased in snow waiting for pickup. The milk had to be watched and guarded, to ensure it was not pilfered.

Four days of milk was lost; it had to be dumped because it exceeded the three-day hold rule. That milk supported two families: mine, consisting of myself, Mom, Dad, and my younger brothers David, Allen, and Randy; and Grandma and Grandpa. Over 10 percent of our income was lost that month. Farming can be unfair because sometimes when you work the hardest you lose the most. I understood that without anyone telling me. I would not ask for anything I did not need for a long time.

My brothers (David, age 10 and Allen, age 9) and I (age 11) shoveled the backyard at the upper farm for turnarounds and a single lane of egress to the street. Randy, at two years old, stayed in the house with Mom. We usually helped Dad with this task. This time we shoveled it ourselves.

"I can't throw it that high!" Allen, as the youngest, always tried to pull his weight, but he was frustrated.

"Aw, come on. You can do it." David and I did not cut our little brother any slack. Allen gave us a hard look and hefted another shovelful of snow. It rolled down the white slope falling to his feet.

"We need to get this shoveled. We can't leave it for Dad." I knew Dad was tired. I had hardly seen him since the blizzard began.

David stood on a low mound he had fashioned. "You can throw it this high. I'll throw it to the top." As my brothers worked their assembly line, I continued to shave slices of snow off the freezing white walls, tossing it so high I could not see it land. When we finished our yard and driveway, we shoveled our neighbors' driveway. Elsie and Dan Worth were older; we knew they could not shovel their driveway themselves.

Our mittens, most knitted by our Aunt Margaret, were repeatedly soaked or iced. We knocked on the closest door for Mom to take them and hand out a dry pair. My fingers wiggled around inside the dry mittens absorbing the warmth they offered. She thawed and dried our things on a collapsible wooden rack placed above the three-foot square heat register in the dining room. Heat radiated through this grate from the coal and wood furnace in the basement. We came inside occasionally during long days of shoveling. I sat on the floor, warming red cold hands and feet above the register until they tingled. We wolfed down a snack Mom had set out, pulled on dry mittens and scurried outside to work on our task.

Mom did not take kindly to dawdling when work was waiting. She had lived on a farm her entire lifetime. Being an only child, though only a youngster during the Great Depression, she was expected to hold her own doing farm chores because Grandpa, her father, could not afford a hired man. Mom also assumed many household duties during the Depression because Grandma worked at the woolen mill in Reedsburg to offset farm expenses. Mom knew from experience what work needed to be done and how long it would take.

My brothers and I were proud we had shoveled the driveways and the entire backyard ourselves. It had taken several days. After the blizzard ended and life settled down, Dad said he was proud of us, too. "I think we should have a picture of you by those mountains of snow so we can remember this blizzard."

We had an extra week of vacation from school because of the Blizzard of 1959.

Carolyn shovels the neighbor's driveway while David and Allen look on from atop the snowpile.

2
Spring Thaw

As days lengthened and temperatures warmed, the snow melted. Spring rains and the thaw caused the ice road to break up and become a huge muddy mess. Gravel for the mostly dirt road was an expensive luxury even though the stone quarry at LaRue was only a couple miles south of the village.

One spring afternoon, a few years before the blizzard, my brothers and I were playing in puddles of melted snow and ice in the half mile road adjacent to our back yard. We picked this special spot because Mom could not easily see us from the house. A row of bridal wreath bushes sprouting leaves partially hid us from her view. Mom constantly told us, "Stay out of the mud."

"Who can splash the highest?" I was the biggest, especially my feet. David could jump the highest. Muddy water went flying. We were wearing five-buckle rubber boots over our shoes. What could possibly happen?

"Stop splashing! You kids get out'a there! You'll be covered with mud!" Allen and I squished water over our boots to rinse away evidence of our play then scampered toward the house. "Carolyn! David! Allen! Get in the house now!"

Allen and I paused. We were not our usual threesome. What? David was not there. We did a quick investigation. David was in the middle of the road crying. That was quite unusual.

"Come on! We'll get in trouble!" We hollered at him.

"I'm stuck in the mud!" David yelled.

"Just step out!"

"I can't!" David, covered with the most mud as usual, had waded out to the deepest part of a big brown puddle before he started squishing muck off his boots. The soft mud was like quicksand. David's weight and his aggressive squishing caused mud at the bottom of the pool to ooze up and over his feet. The murky water was at the very top of his boots. He was a sorry sight. But the situation got worse, much worse.

Mom must have sensed trouble because of our dawdling. She said she had eyes in the back of her head; I swear it was true. When she got to us and surveyed the situation, I saw a momentary twinkle in her eyes. It quickly faded. She could not reach David unless she waded into the puddle. She could not pull on him for fear he might tip over. The puddle was deep. Could he drown?

Mom kicked off her shoes and slogged into the icy-cold water barefoot, hiked her housedress to her rear and got on her knees. She tried to work her hands under David's feet. It was no use. Her hands were red and raw with cold as she dug deep along the front of his legs to unlatch enough buckles to free his feet from the trapped boots. After Mom lugged David out of the large puddle and firmly deposited him on higher ground, she sloshed back into the cold water to retrieve the boots as ripples, then waves, spilled into them because of the agitation.

Allen and I watched this scene wide-eyed and awestruck; we knew the length and volume of Mom's lecture to us would directly increase with the degree of her discomfort. David was traumatized. For him to have allowed himself to get stuck in the mud was humiliating. He knew he would hear this story the rest of his life.

L to R: Allen, Carolyn, and David standing on the west side of the new two-car garage in the backyard of the upper farm. This picture was taken about the same year we were caught splashing in the mud puddles in the half mile road. Our clothes, with the exception of Allen's hat, were handmade by Grandma Hilda Kaun.

3

The First Corner of the Half Mile Road

Our tractors and truck managed navigating the dirt road as the thaw began. However, there were warning signs of impending problems as the road transitioned with the weather. Some especially soft areas grew as wide as a vehicle. When our truck or anything heavy approached an overly soft area of the half mile road, the ground sunk a little and the opposite side of this vulnerable spot rose up. Everyone knew to avoid that stretch of road lest it rupture into a gaping hole of gooey, stinky soup. We could not afford to get vehicles or machinery stuck in the mud.

I did not like to look at the mess after a soft spot broke open. The deep, rolling black muck carried a pungent smell. It was scary, like a dark slimy lizard that could swallow me.

Soft areas usually occurred first at the corner of the road south of our house. There was a phenomenon associated with these spots; we could make the earth move. My brothers and I jumped on the opposite edges of an evolving vulnerable spot. We alternated with each turn, them first with me following close behind.

"You go on that side." David directed. "Allen and I'll stay here. You jump first." I did. The earth sunk a bit below my feet but rose up higher than before when David and Allen jumped on the other side.

"Jump!" David yelled again, and I did.

The soggy soil emitted an increasingly earthy fragrance as we rocked it in the warm sunshine. Like a teeter totter, we could make those spots rise and fall higher and higher. Best if Mom did not catch us doing that, either. When a spot broke open, muck oozed in dark rolls that turned hard as rock as it dried under the bright spring sun. That hard earth had to be broken down and leveled to a smooth surface before our truck and tractors could drive on it.

In years when spring was very wet for an extended time, the village repaired those spots. If they did not, Dad and Grandpa scrimped together enough dollars for a load of gravel to fill the hole. In the meantime, they maneuvered around it by driving on the fields.

A machine shed, chicken coop and rickety corncrib sat at the first corner of the road. They were fenced off from the cow pasture that continued south to the Baraboo River. The threshing machine, silo filler, corn shredder, hay loader, plows, disk and oats binder were stored in that shed. David and Allen raised about a hundred roosters of all varieties in the chicken coop one year. The boys mixed corn mash for the roosters. Their birds thrived and became tasty dinners.

Mom and Dad made a large garden on the corner east of the machine shed and corncrib. Half of the garden was a long bed of strawberries. The other half was planted with cucumbers, tomatoes, squash, beets and carrots. Mom ordered seeds and did the planting. I was about nine years old when I was first expected to weed, pick berries or harvest vegetables by myself.

I did not like the corner garden. It was hot because the machine shed blocked the westerly breeze. The path from the half mile road to the garden was shrouded by tall summer weeds and grasses and curved between the corncrib and a long woodpile. Woodchucks built their nests in the woodpile. I did not like them because they surprised me with their spontaneous scavenging. They waddled between chunks of wood and occasionally peered out to watch me tend the garden.

"Leave the woodchucks alone and they won't bother you. Don't get close. They might get vicious if they think you're going to hurt them." Mom and Dad's advice was not reassuring.

I had a plan in case the woodchucks attacked me or if I saw a snake. My plan was to run and jump into the dilapidated corncrib to escape the danger. To secure my plan, when I first arrived at the corner alone, I checked the wooden latch that held the creaky door of the crib in place. The latch wobbled on a long rusty nail. I escaped to the corncrib a couple times, but in most cases my imagination had caused my fright.

I finished an afternoon of picking strawberries one unseasonably warm day in June. The picking had taken a long time because the berries were small due to the exceptional summer heat and lack of rain. Mom looked perturbed as she inspected the boxes full of puny berries when I pulled them from the wooden carrier and set them on the table. Had I done something wrong?

"Harold, do you have the plow handy?" Mom asked Dad.

"No, but I can get it out. Why?"

"I'm tired of picking a hundred little berries to fill a quart basket and then selling the basket for a quarter when I can buy nice large strawberries for the same price from anyone else."

I did not miss that Mom excluded my contribution of picking the berries, but said nothing.

Dad plowed under the bed of strawberry plants that afternoon.

I smiled. My relief.

4
Iron Country

Looking east from the corner garden, I could see down the half mile road to the fenced-off soggy area that lay between our two farms. Youngstock from the upper barn wandered there in early spring. This small pasture was the upper part of a swale, a shallow depression in the landscape that collected water and slowly released it into the ground. The swale inclined toward the big lowland, along the Baraboo River, that we used as pasture for our dairy cows. In spring the small pasture was a large pool of murky water because surrounding cropland drained into it. It held a collection of puddles all summer except for unusually dry years.

In spring I heard soft "bah-ahs" of youngstock coming from the little pasture. These young cows were transported and spent summers grazing at the Forty, rendering the pasture relatively quiet. We frequently walked between the two farms, except I ran past the little pasture as mosquitoes buzzed my ears and bit my legs and arms. At night a cacophony of frogs burst forth. I heard them from my upstairs bedroom in our farmhouse. On evenings when my room was too warm to sleep, I dragged my bed close to the screened southern window to catch a cool breeze. Many summer evenings I fell asleep to a frog symphony.

One of our artesian wells was located on a slope in the big pasture between our half mile road and the river. This type of well is created by natural underground water pressure and flows without a pump. Artesian wells were common in our area. Water spewed from an eight-inch, rust-covered pipe coming vertically out of the ground, creating a small stream that wound west, then south, through the pasture before emptying into the Baraboo River. We knelt on a piece of damp wood conveniently placed next to the well, bent over and drank the refreshing cold, clear water directly from the pipe. Dad said the water flowed at 34 degrees year around.

The fields immediately north of the well were on higher flat ground and planted with crops of corn, oats and alfalfa or clover that were alternated annually. Dad lowered a couple bottles of beer in a wire basket just below the top of the artesian well pipe when working those fields so he could have a cold one on hot summer days. We were not supposed to tell Mom.

In grade school we read in a Weekly Reader about a cold underground river that came from northern Wisconsin and flowed south. Whether an underground river accounted for the exceptionally cold temperature of the water coming from our artesian wells or not, my family appreciated being able to get a refreshing drink in the field on a hot summer day. I did not mind the iron taste as I slurped. The water was thirst-quenching and cold when we worked the fields or fished the river for northern and bass. We mostly caught carp and bullheads, along with an occasional turtle; once we caught a snake.

Mining companies had been interested in our land years before we owned it. Iron mining retained mineral rights to the property: first the Oliver Mining Company, which was bought out by Bethlehem Steel, which was bought by US Steel when we were just children. Test wells had been drilled, checking for ore early on. They gushed water to ground level unless capped. We were aware of fourteen such test sites on our property. We were not sure of all their exact locations, and there were likely more. Mining companies continued to retain mineral rights when the current owners purchased the property in recent years.

Occasionally a plow or cultivator caught a well cap. This was not good. One day our plow hit a capped well in a field north of the river. Water flew as high as the tractor for several days. We watched land submerge and had to wait for the gusher to subside before capping the well. When water flooded a field, topsoil was eroded. A newly planted field could be ruined because seeds and small plants were washed out of the ground.

When a test well gushed water or started leaking, we took care of the problem quickly to prevent a worse problem. We never considered approaching a mining company and asking them to repair a well. Mining companies retained only the mineral rights to our land, not maintenance of abandoned facilities. One could assume disclosure of capped wells should be included in abstracts. The buyer owns the problems as much as the blessings of the wells. Furthermore, mining companies that dug the test wells on our property no longer existed in the 1950s.

One day a newly planted field close to the lower farm developed a wet spot overnight. We thought an old test well was seeping water. Dad and Grandpa decided to address the situation before it became a disaster. The two men worked together, but did not always get along. A contributing factor to that occasionally strained relationship may have been the fact that each of them had been their own boss for years—Grandpa managing his farm in North Freedom and Dad managing the Schroeder family farm for his mother until he was 36 years old. To his credit, Dad most always gave in to Grandpa, but Dad became crafty in the way he dealt with his father-in-law. Like the way he maneuvered around a confrontation when they had to move milk over the mound of frozen hardpacked snow after the Blizzard of 1959.

When the wet spot appeared in the field, they were compelled to work together to stop the leak. They procured a long chunk of post pole and dug soil to locate and expose the leaking well. The challenge was to position the pole vertically into the open well pipe then drive it deep and solid to stop the flow. I watched from afar as water continued to accumulate in the field.

The smallest end of the hunk of wood was positioned at the top edge of the pipe. Using ropes and props the men heaved with all their might to tip the wooden plug upright. They struggled in mud with the heavy awkward chunk of pole above the well.

"Get in there, you!" The men yelled with each attempt to position and lower the clumsy object into the pipe.

Hydrodynamic pressure caused a geyser gush as flow from the well was restricted. Water shot from around the wood with increased force. The men winced and wiped spray from their eyes as their feet and boots submerged. Water flew higher and higher in all directions as a sledgehammer drove the chunk of pole deep. Dad and Grandpa were soaked in the spraying downpour.

Loud grunts and groans along with occasional swearing were heard between their mighty heaves and heavy pounding.

The tone of their language and length of time it continued scared me. I did not like how they used those "church" words.

As the downpour dwindled, I heard a low throaty gurgle sound. Then I heard it again. Was that Grandpa? Was he laughing?

"By-de...That was..." It was Grandpa's voice dwindling off in the distance.

Then I heard Dad's exhausted chuckle.

Finally, water stopped flowing into the field. Most of the surface water stayed in the area around the pipe where Dad and Grandpa had dug. It evaporated in the warm summer breeze or slowly seeped into the ground. Seeds and small plants sprayed in the downpour soaked up the refreshing drink in short order. The pile of dirt removed from around the well pipe was replaced the following day. Freshly planted seeds and small sprouts of green continued to thrive; few had been lost.

Dad and Grandpa told us they shared a swig of alcohol on the milk house steps before the end of the day to celebrate their success. They did not tell Mom, and we did not share this part of their story with her.

We learned later, the water seeping into this field was from a natural flowing spring that had been capped by the original owners. The water was not from a manmade well. The spring remains plugged.

Looking east, the lower farm is pictured in the distance. The picture was taken from the half mile road by the backyard of the upper farm on the east end of Walnut Street in North Freedom, Wisconsin, in 1966. Farm animals were kept at the lower farm except for the youngstock. Grandma Hilda and Grandpa Louie Kaun were living in the house on the lower farm in 1948 when Harold and Pearl Schroeder, Carolyn (age one), and David (a baby), moved from Caledonia, Minnesota, into the house on the upper place. The house on the lower farm was well built but never had indoor plumbing. The little pasture where frogs and mosquitoes thrived during summer is in the swale in the center of the picture (left of the tree), about a third of the way down the half mile road.

The Upper Farm

Harold Schroeder poses holding Allen in 1952. Carolyn and David are posed on the wide extended axle of the Farmall Model B tractor parked on the half mile road. Our family home on the upper farm is behind the clothesline.

5
Life Along the Railroad Tracks

The Baraboo River wound south and east of our farm, establishing some of the boundaries of our property. It flowed eastward from just south of the first corner of the half mile road, then meandered all the way to the railroad trestle, the bridge of tracks and railroad ties used by the trains to cross the river. The half mile road by our house and a fence extending south to the river bound the west; the railroad tracks bound the north. Originally there were double tracks; the short line from Madison to Cashton had been built to haul farm supplies and freight. Chicago & Northwestern passenger trains were regular modes of travel and also carried mail for the US Postal Service. Hopper cars hauled quartzite from area quarries. Circus trains in summer were the most exciting: flat cars carried bright-colored wagons and cages. We could see animals in some of the cages from our yard, but it was hard to make out which animals they were. Fewer circus trains passed by with the demise of small circus companies until there were none.

 Mom and Dad first warned us about the dangers of living close to the railroad tracks when we were very young. Dad's warnings were serious and direct. "Don't ever walk on the railroad tracks. If for any reason a person fell and bumped their head and passed out or laid down and fell asleep on the tracks, they could be hit by a train or one of the small handcars." Handcars were small open flatbeds with room for only a couple rail inspectors. Most were pumped by hand and thus rolled along quietly; others were motorized.

"The handcars are little, and they don't go by very often," I piped up.

"That makes them more dangerous because you won't expect to see one. Plus, they don't make a loud warning noise like the trains."

Dad's warnings continued: "The trestle is dangerous because you could fall through the open places between the railroad ties. You can't run across the open ties. If you're caught off guard in the middle of the trestle, you could be hit by a train and seriously injured. No one would hear a call for help. It's too far from either farm." At seven years old, I seriously absorbed Dad's every word. I had never seen the trestle, but knew it was built across the river, beyond the lower farm.

Within a couple years, David and Allen were sent across the trestle to gather asparagus. Dad warned them not to venture as far as the rock cut on the east side of the river. The rock cut was a spot where hobos spent the night when the weather was tolerable. When temperatures dropped, hobos could be found warming themselves at the train depot uptown until they were shooed out. Dad sometimes offered them a job when he was shorthanded on the farm, but the hobos said they were not interested. They preferred their nomadic lifestyle.

One day when we were alone, Dad told me, again, not to walk on the trestle. He said my rules were different than those for my brothers. To get to the trestle, you had to cross the boundary fence at the most eastern edge of our property and walk across a short piece of Dickie's land.

Lincoln Dickie owned the property on all four sides of the trestle. His farmland was on the north side of the tracks, east of Shimniok's property. He also owned small pieces of land by the trestle on our side of the tracks. It is likely the railroad wanted it that way because they dealt with only one land owner when work had to be done on the trestle.

A strange feeling spread through me the first time I walked across the trestle watching the muddy water far below. It was less like fear and more like guilt for not heeding Dad's warning. I was 11 years old and had been cultivating corn in the field closest to the trestle when I had a compelling desire to walk across it—alone. I never told anyone.

Mom and Dad told us about hobos that rode the rails. They explained these homeless travelers usually meant no harm. I saw them during summer in their scraggly, dirty clothes and grimy skin when they came to our door looking for food or a drink. Mom accommodated them, but they were not invited or allowed into the house.

Occasionally, there was a rap at one of the screen doors, when I was alone in the house because Mom was elsewhere on the farm. The rapping was unusual because we almost always knew when someone was coming to our home. I could easily peer toward both the front and back doors from anywhere in the house. When I saw a hobo knocking, I froze. Sometimes, they called out. I never answered and felt safest not moving until they left. When I told Mom, she said, "That's the best thing for you to do. I don't want you to open our doors for hobos. It's okay for me to help them, but they should not be talking to a child."

Some people talked about putting coins on the tracks. They said the weight of the train would squish a coin and make it thin, flat and much bigger. Dad said, "Coins on the railroad tracks could cause a problem with a train that

North Freedom

could be disastrous." I thought he was exaggerating but never considered contradicting him. I think it was his way of discouraging us from going by the tracks and from wasting money.

Mom reinforced Dad's point. "If you have money to waste by putting it on the railroad tracks, I'll take it. Plus, you'll lose your allowance."

One thing about living close to the tracks was the noise: the engines, the rattle of locomotives and cars, and the warning whistle as the train approached the crossing at Walnut Street to alert traffic and the station. Our house was about a hundred yards from the tracks; Elsie and Dan's house was in between. The ground vibrated when trains passed by, making Mom's best crystal goblets, the ones we hardly ever used, softly clink against each other in the narrow wall cabinets in the dining room. We grew so accustomed to train noise, sometimes we did not hear it at all. One time a different noise surprised Mom.

Mom took a nap in her chair one afternoon because she had been up with Randy, our little brother, most of the night, as he had a chronic ear infection. A long quarry train rumbled into town while she slept. The usual train noise did not bother Mom as she continued sleeping soundly.

Near her chair was a marble ramp toy that our great uncle Rudy, Grandma Hilda's stepbrother, had made for us. It was painted red and had five narrow wooden troughs that Rudy whittled just wide enough to hold a marble. The troughs were positioned at ever increasing angles between two vertical pieces of wood. There was a little box attached to catch marbles at the end of the last run. We rolled small marbles from our Chinese checkers game down the contraption because big marbles from our bags occasionally got stuck and plugged the transitions between the troughs.

The marble ramp toy, sitting directly behind Mom as she slept in her chair with the train rumbling by, had one of our fat marbles stuck in the first transition. 10 or more small marbles were stuck behind the fat marble. The long quarry train continued to rumble until the vibration shook the fat marble lose. Mom's ears were not accustomed to this strange sound. She roused and was startled when she heard the "plink, swish, plink, swish" sound. Faster and faster the marbles fell.

"Someone is in the house!" Mom's eyes flew wide open as she tried to get her bearings. When the little marbles were freed, they followed the fat marble and dropped through the transition one after the other. The fat marble picked up speed and tore through the next two transitions followed by the speedy little marbles. At the last transition, the fat marble was screaming along with the little marbles in hot pursuit. "Whiz! Whiz! Whiz!" And at the end, "Plop. Plop. Plop."

Mom screamed, too; tiny little "Ah, Ah, Ah" screams at first, followed by "Oh! Oh! Help! Help!" screams and shouts. She was sure whatever was in the house was on the move, faster and faster.

Mom was embarrassed when she discovered it was the marble game that had scared her. She probably would not have told the story if no one heard her holler, but she could not be sure. She thought she best make light of the situation and laugh about it. She admitted she was relieved, too.

Mail was transported in canvas bags on the three o'clock passenger train. It was sorted on the train, so when it arrived at the post office, it was available in short order. When there was no other reason to stop, the mailbag of incoming mail was simply dropped from the train at the small depot south of the tracks on the west side of Depot Street. In the early days, old Dan Seeley picked up the canvas bag, hefted it onto an ancient steel-wheeled wooden cart and pushed it two blocks to the post office uptown. The outgoing mail was hung on a hook at the depot and grabbed as the train passed by. Parcel post packages normally required the train to stop, depending on the size and content—like when a box of our peeping baby chicks arrived.

Old Dan Seeley collected the mail for years. Dan and Mary were our neighbors on the east end of Walnut Street. They lived in the half-painted house across the half mile road from us. Dan Seeley's large lot extended south of Walnut Street all the way to the first corner of the half mile road. Grandpa said Dan was a prominent citizen and leader in the village in his early days.

"Dan Seeley died." I was five years old when Mom told me this. I did not know what I should say, so I said nothing as I experienced my first eerie encounter with death.

There were indications of coming technology after Dan stopped collecting mail. Bill Born first picked up the mail using a motor vehicle in place of the pushcart used by Dan. Later, when transporting the mail changed from train to truck, Mom shook her head with dismay. "Well, Bill Born is out of a job." She went on to explain her concern was not only for Mr. Born but also for what this change meant for the railroad industry and the country in general.

Grandma Hilda took the train from North Freedom to Reedsburg to visit her sisters Martha, Emma, and her half-sister, Alma. Reedsburg was 12 miles to the northwest. Allen accompanied Grandma one day as a special treat. She told Allen to watch the mailbag on the hook as an eastbound train approached the depot. Allen was still excited when he told me, "A hand came out of the train car and grabbed the bag." I went to Reedsburg on that train by myself a number of times and saw the eastbound come into town. I observed the mailbag hanging in the air but was always disappointed because I never saw a grab.

I was only eight years old the first time I rode the train to Reedsburg alone to visit my aunts. I imitated the persona of adult passengers, determined to hide my insecurity which was short lived with experience. A year after that first trip, Mom and Martha arranged for me to accompany Martha on the Chicago & Northwestern 400 train to Madison, the capital of Wisconsin. She was visiting Rudy and his wife, Mandy.

It was a long ride, and I watched with interest as passengers were dropped off and others picked up at stops along the 50-mile route. Our easy conversation was abruptly interrupted when Martha's eye caught something on the horizon. "Look." Martha pointed to the distinctive dome in the distance as we approached the city. This was the first time I saw the capitol building.

Rudy and Mandy lived close to the railroad tracks between Lake Monona and the State Capitol Building sitting on the isthmus, that narrow strip of land between Lake Monona and Lake Mendota that served as the foundation for the impressive domed structure. The tracks ran close to the water so we had a short climb to their home on Franklin Street. I did not mind the exercise after the long train ride because I knew a plate of Mandy's fresh baked cookies would be on the small table sitting in the hallway.

I wrote letters to Martha a couple times each year, starting when I could put a sentence together. Martha kept the letters she liked best and gave them back to me at one special wedding shower. In one of those I wrote "Mom cnt me to the selr four potpoes..." which translated to "Mom sent me to the cellar for potatoes." The best part was when Martha wrote back. I thought of this years later when I heard how much soldiers enjoy receiving mail.

Picking up the daily mail in the 1950s was an event, because mail was the primary means of communication. Many people, including our family, did not have a telephone. We got our first telephone in 1959; I was 11 years old. We were on a party line with two other households using the same line.

After the mail train passed each day, Mom sent one of us to walk the four blocks to the post office uptown. When it was my turn, I saw neighbors and classmates on my way. Sometimes Mom had all three of us kids in the car and stopped by the post office where she directed one of us to get the mail. Folks from the village were in the lobby in front of the wall of metal boxes. We rented box number 251 in the old post office in the big brick building on the southeast corner of Walnut and Maple Street uptown. My earliest memories are using a key to open our mailbox before they were upgraded with dial locks. Sometimes there was a note with our mail saying we had a parcel or postage was due. We took those notes to Bob Myers, the postmaster, to collect our package or pay our bill. When the post office moved across the street in the mid-1950s, we were assigned mailbox 86; it had a different combination.

Bob Myers always had a friendly and sometimes humorous greeting. He liked to make up rhyming salutations using kids' names. Bob said to my classmate, "Sandy, Sandy she's so handy." Bob's daughter's name was Carolyn, the same as mine. She was my best friend. When Bob saw me, he usually said, "Hello there, young lady." I think he did not have words to rhyme with Carolyn.

Carolyn and I played with her dolls and danced to music played on her small portable phonograph in her bedroom on the second floor of the Myers' home across the street from the grade school. My mom and Rose, Carolyn's mother, arranged these playtimes, the only ones I ever had.

One very cold winter day Mom told me not to walk home from school; she would pick me up in the car. I was in first grade; my brothers were too young for school. When classes were released at the end of the day, Mom was not waiting for me in the car. Carolyn asked me to come to her house to wait and stay warm. I thought this was a wonderful idea. I told Rose I was sure Mom would not mind because of our previous playdates.

Carolyn and I were having a great time with her dolls and listening to music when we heard this commotion downstairs. Mom's voice. "Is she here? I was so worried." Rose was apologizing. Mom had apparently gone into the school looking for me and a number of people got involved in the search. I was in big trouble and terrified I would never be allowed to play with Carolyn again. In retrospect, now having children and grandchildren of my own, I better understand Mom's fear in not being able to locate me. Yes, I was allowed more playtime with Carolyn but had to ask Mom's permission. When Carolyn was my guest, we played board games, or croquet on the front lawn with my brothers.

Bob and Rose Myers did their grocery shopping on Friday evenings in Baraboo. Occasionally, I was asked to accompany them. Mom and Dad seldom went to the bigger grocery stores outside of North Freedom because we ate food from our farm. We two Carolyns went to Woolworth's dime store those Friday nights and mulled over the selection of books, art supplies, scarves, hair ties and barrettes as well as the huge selection of candy. Some of my allowance was stashed in my pocketbook; this I managed as I made selections for purchase. These evenings ended with a cone at the Tastee Freez.

Bob Myers organized an event for a sizable group in Wisconsin Dells one summer, an Upper Dells boat trip on the Wisconsin River. A couple of girls were needed to serve snacks and beverages; Carolyn and I were asked to assist. This was a big treat for me, not work.

Bob and Rose also took Carolyn and me to Tommy Bartlett's Water Ski and Jumping Boat Thrill Show in Wisconsin Dells. One summer, performers from the Lawrence Welk Show were featured performers. We saw the Lennon Sisters. After listening to their harmony, Carolyn and I met them as we exited the grounds. Later in the summer Jo Ann Castle, on the honky-tonk piano, was part of the show.

My experiences with the Myers family and Carolyn's friendship opened doors for me that may otherwise have been closed because of the responsibilities Mom and Dad had with the farm and my younger brothers. However, I knew the security of my family was waiting each time I crossed the railroad tracks upon returning to North Freedom.

"The last steam train will be going by about now." Grandpa's growly voice made the announcement. We could already hear the whistle blasting. David and I scrambled to the kitchen window for the best view of the tracks. Allen could not see around us so Grandpa scooped him up to watch above our heads as a steam train rumbled through North Freedom for the last time in the early 1950s. After that day locomotives passing by were powered with diesel engines.

6

Laundry

Laundry was an all-day event. There was not an exact day designated as laundry day. Rather it was more weather dependent. Mom considered the direction the wind was blowing before she started washing clothes. This was because we lived close to the railroad tracks; black smoke blew from steam locomotives that passed by daily. The usual westerly wind was no problem, but when the wind blew from the northeast on laundry day and Mom's sharp ears heard the warning whistle of an approaching train, she yelled, "Get the clothes! The train's coming!"

    I dropped what I was doing and ran. Whites were pulled first. Nothing was neatly folded or sorted like usual. If we were too late there would be black specks of soot all over our freshly washed clothes. When that happened, Mom rewashed only our best white clothes and tablecloths to remove the black. The rest was worn or used, soot and all.

    When the last steam train rolled through North Freedom that problem ended—only to rise again in 1963 when the Mid-Continent Railroad Museum moved to town and initially planned to use the North Freedom Depot. Complaints were quickly squelched when the museum acquired the Chicago & Northwestern depot in Rock Springs and moved it to its present site west of the village.

Pulling laundry was most difficult during the winter because it froze on the line. It was then that I quickly pulled clothespins, shoving as many as possible into my mouth. Stiff sheets, towels and overalls were bent. I fit as many pieces as possible into the clothesbasket and stuffed more under one arm. Fingers, numb with cold, awkwardly wheedled the first few clothespins from my mouth, often causing cracked and bleeding lips.

Frozen clothes would dry outside. The result was the freshest smelling laundry ever. However, it took longer to dry clothes in freezing temperatures. Early winter sunsets happening around four o'clock meant laundry often had to be taken into the house still damp or frozen because Mom did not want laundry on the line overnight.

Frozen laundry quickly melted once inside the house. The result was a mound of damp clothes and linens that were draped over collapsible wooden racks by the heat register in the dining room. If too many layers of wet laundry ended up on the clothes racks, it did not dry properly and the sour smell of stale laundry lingered until next washday. I occasionally recalled that smell in a warm classroom and wondered if it was coming from me or from another classmate who had to wear sour stale clothes.

Our laundry was in the cellar. This area was known as the cellar until we started calling it the basement when I was in the upper grades. The only entrance and egress was a set of steep wooden stairs. There were two doors at the narrow landing at the top of those stairs. One was the outside door to the backyard; the other was the door to the bathroom leading into the house. At the bottom of the stairs was a sharp left turn and another couple steps to the cement floor of the combination laundry room and furnace area.

We had an electric wringer washing machine, two rinse tubs, a sink with hot and cold water faucets, and wooden shelves by the sink for a box of granulated powder soap and a wooden wash stick. There were several slat wood laundry baskets with wire handles, lined with oilcloth printed with red flowers on a white background.

The furnace sat at the bottom of the stairs. A series of hooks on the wall across from the furnace held Dad's overalls and seasonal work clothes. Clean overalls were hung separately from overalls that had seen barn or field duty. The amount of mud and manure on a pair of overalls indicated the number of times they had been worn, the type of work the men were doing and weather conditions.

There were always a couple extra clean overalls for guests choosing to join Dad during milking time. Cows were milked every twelve hours. Cows give less milk if milking schedules change, so when company stayed until milking time, our guests were given the opportunity to go to the barn with Dad or stay in the house. Dad's brothers, relatives and friends from Caledonia, Minnesota, were most likely to go to the barn with Dad. Mom's relatives usually stayed in the house. Women guests did not go to the barn except my cousin Tom Schroeder's daughter, Jonette. She loved farming.

The washing machine and rinse tubs were stored along the west side of the room along the stone room-dividing wall and pulled to the center of the floor for laundry day. Mom filled the machine with hot water by connecting a hose to the faucet. A week of dirty laundry was sorted into seven or eight piles on the floor. The same water was used for all loads. Whites and linens were washed first. Then followed in order: light colored clothes, the cleanest colored clothes, the dirtier colored clothes, overalls we kids wore for farm work and finally Dad's overalls. The last loads were nasty because they usually had mud and cow, pig or chicken manure on them. If the overalls were extremely filthy, we hauled them outside along with a five-gallon pail of water and scrubbed off mud and manure using a sturdy brush before placing the overalls in the washing machine.

Laundry powder was added and dissolved in the steamy water while the agitator was moving followed by a load of whites that churned in the tub for about five minutes. After the agitator stopped, a wash stick about 20 inches long and an inch in diameter was used to lift the first loads out of hot water and guide them through the wringer into the first rinse tub on the other side. Large pieces like bedding and bulky pieces like overalls needed special attention.

The wringer was about 14 inches wide, and when locked in place, two rotating rollers squeezed water out of material as it was fed between them. If the material was too thick, the lock released and the rollers stopped. When this happened, the partially wrung material had to be manually backed out of the rollers, the wringer reset and the process restarted. A corner of a sheet was fed into the wringer first. The usual twists in the steaming sheets were undone as the material fed through the rollers. Sometimes they were put through the wringer twice to squeeze out more water. Collars of individual shirts and waistbands of jeans were fed between the rollers with the rest of each garment following to minimize wrinkles.

Mom did the first loads because the water was steamy hot, making the cumbersome sheets difficult to handle. When I took over loads of colored clothes, I used the wash stick to find little pieces like underwear, socks and handkerchiefs. Several small items were run through the wringer together because it did not exert enough pressure to remove water from a single small item. The wringer was optimized and set to accommodate all items large and small. We washed many handkerchiefs, the classic red or blue and white, some with fancy embroidery or cut work, and many colors and prints. We blew our noses and wiped our brows with handkerchiefs. There were no disposable tissues.

Mounds of fluffy soapsuds prevented seeing what was in the washing machine at the beginning of the process. Each load added its own murkiness to the water that was already a light shade of gray by the time the first coloreds were washed. Eventually the bubbles disappeared and the water got so murky it was impossible to see through it. Mom finished Dad's overalls because they were difficult to get through the wringer without having it release.

"We're lucky to have a wringer with a release because if someone, especially a little girl or boy, got their hand caught in a wringer without a release, the wringer could take their arm off, or worse." One day I asked Mom what "worse" was because I expected she was exaggerating. She looked me straight in the eye like she did not want to explain. "Worse is getting their skin pulled away from the bone or pulling their whole body through the wringer." Her reply was so serious; I wondered. Had she experienced such a dreadful scene? That kind of answer taught me not to question Mom.

Every load was rinsed in both galvanized tubs going through the wringer each time. The wringer was swung clockwise and locked in place to accommodate wringing between each of the tubs and finally into the clothesbasket.

Wet clothes were carried up the stairs, across the lawn and hung on the clothesline using slotted wooden pins from the pin basket.

Mom had rules about hanging laundry. Clotheslines were wiped clean for linens and church and school clothes, but lines for overalls were seldom wiped. Sheets and pillowcases went on the first line because it was most visible from Walnut Street. Underwear was hung behind sheets, hidden from view. Clothes were hung overlapping so clothespins could be shared; each item did not need two pins. Shirts were hung by the vertical seam on either side of the tail. Pants and overalls were hung by the bottom, not the waist. Clothespins were either holding clothes or in the pin basket, not left on the lines. The pin basket was brought into the house with the last basket of clean laundry.

Wash water was dark gray, almost black, when the last load of laundry was done. There was no drain in the basement so water in the washing machine and the two rinse tubs had to be hauled outside. I lugged five-gallon buckets up the basement steps, down the sloping sidewalk, along the new garage and dumped them on the ground at the end of the cement. The object was to complete the job with the fewest trips while carrying buckets filled with volumes I could manage.

Occasionally a bucket of water was dropped on the stairs. This mess had to be cleaned because a wet spot in the basement could create a musty, moldy smell throughout the entire house. It was dark behind the steps because the stairs blocked light from the single bulb in the ceiling above the upper landing. Spider webs and thick dust balls lurked there. To clean up the water I had to maneuver between the narrow storage shelves holding canning supplies and the open edge of the steps to get behind the stairs. I got on my knees and worked as fast as I could with rags and a small bucket to sop up and wring out the slimy goo. When the floor started to dry, a sturdy goose feather brush pushed dirt and debris onto a piece of newspaper to finish the job. Goose feather brushes were the end of goose wing from the outermost joint to the tip, and were excellent tools for cleaning small messes.

A layer of dark gray muck coagulated on the bottom of the washing machine even if water was stirred as the tub drained. I used old towels to clean the sides of the machine and slopped sludge from under the agitator, then rinsed the tub with clean water and wiped it dry so it was ready for next laundry day. If this was not done promptly it created a terrible stink.

Winter made laundry more challenging. A couple inches of ice usually formed on the cement steps outside the basement door because of melting and freezing caused by the warm inside and the cold outside. A few icicles on the eave above the steps dripped during the day to thicken the ice and make the top of the steps round and slick when the sun went down. The walk had to be shoveled all the way to the end of the garage about eighty feet. The sidewalk sloped south from the basement door. Sunshine melted snow during the day making little streams of water on the cement that became slippery black ice when the sun set. It was usually dark when I started carrying wash water in freezing temperatures because of the short periods of daylight during Wisconsin winters.

I faced a tradeoff between wearing my warm winter coat or leaving it off. If I put it on, I could stay warm outside and sweat in the basement as the tubs slowly drained. If I skipped it, I could dawdle with my back against the warm furnace soaking up enough heat to last as I struggled buckets up the steps, sloshed along the walk, dumped the water and slip-slided back to the house. Frozen fingers were a hazard whatever I did because gloves and mittens always got wet.

Sometimes I did not finish emptying the washtubs, but it was not intentional. I was needed elsewhere for other tasks: cooking, helping with my baby brother, shoveling snow, barn chores or harvesting. Dad washed at the sink in the basement after he finished evening milking and fieldwork. If I had not finished carrying the water, he hauled it up the stairs and cleaned the tubs. The first time I left wash water for Dad, I felt guilty and ran to the basement when he came in from chores. I knew he read my thoughts because he smiled at me when he said, "It's okay, Susie." Dad did not complain or reprimand me which made me feel worse.

Dad started calling me Susie in the early 1950s when the song and phrase Susie Q was popular. My brothers still call me Susie on occasion, mostly to tease.

7

The Rest of the Basement

All outer walls of the cellar were stone, including a partition between the laundry room and the west part of the basement. Two windows were fashioned into the stone foundation on the south side of the farmhouse. They filtered in limited sunlight but did not open and were so small only a child would fit through. One of those windows was in the laundry room.

The furnace sat toward the north side of the laundry room; the small coal bin and wood room was beyond. A wooden partition had been constructed between the furnace and the coal bin. There was no window in the coal bin, only a hatch on the north wall about two feet square.

Sometimes Dad bought a truckload or two of wood slabs from the railroad tie sawmill on Maple Hill, about four miles southwest of our farm. This area was one of the original settlements in the Town of Freedom. Dad parked the truck loaded with wood in the drive on the north side of the house. My brothers and I tossed the slabs from the truck bed to the ground, and then from the ground through the small hatch into the coal bin. Work gloves, if available, prevented slivers.

"Look, I can throw a piece straight from here into the hatch," David bragged. He was standing on the bed of the truck and was now strong enough to launch the awkward pieces. His natural aim resulted in a quiet swish of wood through the hatch. Being the oldest, bigger and taller than David, I was not about to let him out do me.

Thwack! I had selected a large chunk of wood that promptly hit the house when I threw it. I tried a smaller piece. Thwack! I was about to launch a third, sure I would hit the hatch this time, when I heard, "What's going on out there." Mom did not like hearing the thwacks because she knew they could leave marks on the wood siding around the hatch.

With concentrated practice and when Mom was not in the house, I got pretty good at throwing a piece of wood from the truck and hitting the narrow hatch, eliminating a step, just like my brother. This skill took less than a week to perfect. The task was good training for my baseball skills used later on the ball diamond at the grade school uptown.

More than once my brothers and I accidently hit each other with a slab of wood causing a lump on the head, a black eye or a nosebleed. As slabs of wood accumulated in the basement, we ranked them along the walls to make room for a couple tons of coal.

The west part of the cellar was used as a large fruit room when our family first moved into the house; this type of room was also known as a root cellar. We did not need all of the large fruit room for food, so Dad built a partition to split off and retain a small closet-sized fruit room on the north side. The remaining larger area became our playroom.

The stone walls were fashioned to create a freeform stone shelf around the south and west sides of the room. The shelf was shoulder high. A shaft of sunlight filtered in through the small window. Mom and Dad spray painted the walls and ceiling of the playroom a rosy pink tan using the old Kenmore vacuum cleaner for the compressor and its pintsize Mason jar attachment for the sprayer. It actually worked quite well.

Dad called my brothers and me together when his measuring and hammering and the painting was finished. "This room is for you," he explained.

At five, six and seven years old, my brothers and I were not sure what Dad meant. "What are we supposed to do with it?" we asked.

"This is your own place. To play." Dad stressed the room was our own place. He also stressed if we could not get along and share the room nicely, he and Mom would take the room back. We stood there not sure what to do. However, it did not take long to get over the shock of having a place of our own and quickly brought our meager collection of treasures to the cellar, unsupervised. We each staked a collectively agreed upon area to claim as our own.

The few toys we had were mostly used or broken and required imagination for play. Many of these toys were bought by the bushel basket or box at local auctions. Sometimes Dad bought a whole bushel of toys for 50 cents. A few of those were good, but many were broken. We had a small cylinder of tinker toys, just enough to make a windmill that did not turn. There was an old incomplete and a newer full set of Lincoln Logs. They were not totally compatible because one set had round ended logs and the other square ended logs. They made for interesting lopsided buildings. There was an electric train, tracks and cars we put together for pretend, but we quickly lost interest because it never worked. There were jigsaw puzzles and games: checkers, Chinese checkers, Parcheesi and eventually a Monopoly game. Mostly we made our own adventure games with boxes, an ancient card table and old holey flannel blankets for forts and hills. Sometimes we made up skits to perform when relatives visited.

After several weeks of play, the room was in such disarray it became difficult to wade through the clutter. We cleaned the room on our own to make a new backdrop for the next adventure. There was no adult supervision when we were in our playroom. It was ours. We had some terrific fights in the basement. None were serious enough to come to blows; their cause was not remembered. We sorted our differences on our own, knowing it was best not to involve our parents. We knew that tattling or too much hollering resulted with all of us in trouble and the end of playtime.

The small fruit room on the north side of the playroom had shelves for the food we canned during summer: vegetables, fruit, soup, juice, pickles and much more. There were gunny sacks of potatoes and onions on the floor. During the year I was sent to the fruit room to bring food to the kitchen. There were no lights in this small storage area. We owned one flashlight, but it was seldom in the fruit room. To compensate for this lack of light, items were consistently stored in their specific place in the little room. I had the storage layout memorized by the time I started school.

Mom sent us to the basement daily for food. When she said, "Get some potatoes" or "Get some onions," I grabbed the large white enamel pan with the red rim and headed for the fruit room.

It had its own peculiar odor from many years of storing food and dripping or broken jars. When the odor changed to rank and pungent, I knew there was at least one rotten potato or onion in a gunny sack lying on the floor. The first time I stuck my hand into a rotten potato in the dark I almost threw up. I had to clean the mess. I smelled that stench and saw that yuck for days. After that experience, I more cautiously approached the potato sack on the floor. I held the sack open with one hand and felt the outside of the scratchy material with my other hand to find a solid potato. One good potato gave me confidence to check the next potato with one finger. I never put my whole hand into a rotten potato or onion again. But I laughed when it happened to my brothers.

During the Cold War, our family determined the fruit room would be our fallout shelter in case of an enemy attack or atomic bomb.

Dad made wine in gray ceramic crocks and jugs that sat on the basement floor. There was a long fence of concord grapevines by the garden at the lower farm. His wine making increased when Grandma Hilda and Grandpa Louie moved from the house on the lower farm to their home on Franklin Street, a block toward uptown from our place. Their new house had a wooden fence also laden with vines of beautiful dark blue-purple grapes. Dad said, "We can't possibly eat all these grapes." He shook his head, but smiled with his idea. "It would be a shame to waste them. I think I should make a little more wine."

Dad also made wine from the wild grapes growing by the large black walnut tree at the first corner of the half mile road and elderberries growing along the western fence of our property. The pungent smell coming from the crocks made it hard to presume something smelling that awful could possibly taste good. After his wine fermented, Dad gave a tiny sample of the deep red liquid to me in a small glass. It tasted yucky, but he and other relatives enjoyed it. Mom did not drink alcohol.

Mom made sweet pickles in small crocks in the basement. I was not fond of sweet pickles as a kid. It was probably a good thing my brothers and I found neither the wine nor the pickles appealing. We left the crocks alone except when something from our play landed in one and had to be fished out of the sticky liquid.

There were a few granddaddy long leg spiders in the cellar. They lurked in dark corners, but ventured out to surprise me by crawling along my arm, leg or neck. A swift long swipe flung them away—somewhere—but I was quite sure they were still alive and waiting to seek their vengeance by landing on me again. Their long legs made them feel like there were eight crawlies on my skin, not one spider with eight long legs. Smaller spiders also hid in the corners, but they were less likely to wander out and bother me.

A crop of crickets appeared in the cellar spontaneously on a regular basis. Like the spiders, they hid away in dark corners. We had a great cricket plague one year when they filled the foundation walls of the house. It began with the typical annual crop of crickets chirping away in the corners. This particular year their number increased dramatically and they jumped out from their hiding places because there were so many they had nowhere to go. Some crawled from the foundation into the rooms upstairs.

"You kids go down cellar and stomp out the crickets." Mom was fretting because she did not want to have to explain our cricket issue to her relatives who were coming for the usual Saturday night card playing ritual.

My brothers and I did our best with the crickets, but every time we stomped one, another took its place. And—they were getting bigger. Many were well over an inch long.

"We stomped a bunch of crickets, but there're more down there," we reported to Mom.

Mom mentioned the crickets in an offhanded way when our relatives arrived on Saturday. The crickets were multiplying in the cellar below the living room and dining room. Card playing happened in the dining room and kitchen. Mom was hoping for the best.

Allen and I were told to sit in the living room and kick rogue crickets under the couch. (Mom did not want them squished on the new green carpeting.) My cheeks were red with embarrassment when I had to deal with errant crickets that evening.

The following week, Mom had Allen spray around the outside foundation of the house using the small hand pump sprayer with farm pesticide in the tank. Thousands of crickets jumped into the cellar to escape the deadly fumes. They died on the floor and crunched when we walked on them. We used a small shovel to scoop their little bodies into a five-gallon pail for disposal. After that fiasco, we sprayed from inside the house, not from the outside, when dealing with crickets.

8

Bathroom

At the top of the basement stairs was a door to our bathroom: toilet, small sink and claw foot tub. "Get a kiss. Daddy's going outside." My brothers and I ran from whatever we were doing through the bathroom to the door where Dad stood at the top of the basement stairs waiting for us to give him a kiss before he left. The thought reminds me of the mingled fragrance of pipe tobacco and Old Spice aftershave. Our bathroom had three doors: the one to the basement, the door to the kitchen and one into Mom and Dad's bedroom. Our old farmhouse was built with no indoor plumbing. Later, but before we moved in, an existing pantry was converted into a bathroom. However, a bathroom with three doors presents privacy problems.

None of the existing doors had locks, so hook and eye latches were installed. Mom and Dad said if a door was closed, we were to politely call "Is someone in the bathroom?" before entering. This led to another problem. The person leaving the locked bathroom usually unlocked only the door they exited. Mom constantly reminded us, "Unlock all the doors when you leave the bathroom."

The hook and eye system worked until someone had to go really bad. They were usually in a hurry, called out, waited briefly, then pushed through the closed door that likely was hooked shut. Bam! Clink! The hook and eye pulled straight out of the wood and bounced off the sink, toilet or tub. Frustrated, Mom located and repositioned the hook and eye. This worked briefly, but soon Bam! Clink! The wooden doors were being destroyed.

"There are no locks on the bathroom doors." Mom made the announcement at supper one night. "Anyone wanting privacy in the bathroom has to make noise: sing, count, talk. If you hear someone in the bathroom, don't go in. Either wait your turn or use the outhouse." Dad and the boys were encouraged to use the outhouse during the summer. The stated reason was to save water. However, no one believed that was the real reason.

Bath water was not changed between our baths. I was lucky being the only girl because I had the privilege to bathe first. Then David and Allen went in the tub together until they got too big. Dad was last. Hot water was added between each bath for a comfortable temperature. Mom usually bathed in fresh water after everyone else was in bed.

The older I got, the more noise I made in the bathroom.

9

Kitchen

The kitchen was small. One end of the table was pushed tightly against the wall on the north side of the room so it did not block the door to the dining room. My brothers and I sat on an old oilcloth covered piano bench slid against the west and north walls. The bench allowed us to sit high at the small table without falling. It was like a booster seat for three. David and I had to lift and push Allen's behind onto the bench until he was big enough to climb onto it himself. Dad sat at the head of the table; Mom sat across from us kids so she had handy access to the entire kitchen.

    I was nine years old when my youngest brother, Randy, joined us at the corner of the table between Mom and Dad. He sat in the old wooden highchair we had all used. Mom sat in it first when she was a baby. The highchair served a dual purpose: when we made noodles, we hung the long thin strips of soft flattened dough on a towel draped over the back of the highchair until they dried.

    A big enclosed porch was off the kitchen. During the summer we ate on the porch where screened windows to the south and east provided a comfortable breeze. We had one small table fan. It was usually in Mom and Dad's bedroom. On hot humid days it was moved to the porch during mealtimes. I would sneak brief moments from daily tasks to stand in front of the fan where the refreshing breeze evaporated perspiration on my forehead and scattered the tight ringlets of my curly hair. Closing my eyes, I vowed someday I would have my very own fan so I would never be so uncomfortable.

This little farmhouse kitchen was the work center of our home. It had a gas stove. I learned to light the burners when I was about 10 years old by turning on the gas to a low hissing stream, then striking a match along the grate.

Mom made all entrees and side dishes on top of the stove. She made tasty tender beef roasts from the oldest, toughest cuts of meat from our butchering by browning the meat in a heavy five-quart roasting pan she called a Dutch oven, then lowering the flame and letting it simmer for hours, frequently adding small amounts of water. "Catch the roast, Susie," was my cue to add water and loosen the brown drippings from the bottom of the pan. I learned a rich beefy aroma was triggered when the roast needed water, and Mom no longer needed to remind me. The oven was used to bake cookies, sheet cakes, pies and bars. Our small refrigerator had a tiny freezer about a foot square. It held two trays of ice cubes along with an occasional quart of ice cream.

When I was 12, Mom and Dad felt my brothers and I were old enough to stay alone while they attended a midday cooperative meeting in Reedsburg. The tasks we were assigned in their absence were quickly accomplished, and I imagined wonderful things I could do the rest of the day. Ultimately, Allen and I decided to surprise Mom and Dad and make a white layer cake. We had been impressed with these beautiful cakes at weddings and anniversaries, but they were something Mom did not fuss with.

It took a while to find a recipe. We set two round pans and all the ingredients on the table except one. The recipe called for shortening. We had lard and butter, but there was nothing called shortening in the cupboard. Mom kept a jar of greasy stuff in the refrigerator that she used to scoop into a pan to fry meat or potatoes. Allen and I decided we could use it as shortening in our cake knowing Mom frequently substituted ingredients.

"I'll light the oven." I was the oldest and Mom had shown me how to turn on the gas and how to strike a match and hold the flame directly above the little hole in the bottom of the oven, but I had never done it myself. I was nervous until I heard the swish of the big burner lighting.

The cake turned out perfect and was cooling in the pans when Mom and Dad returned. "What a wonderful surprise. I'll make some frosting. We'll have cake for dessert after supper." Mom was already hauling ingredients to the table.

"We used your grease for shortening," Allen and I explained to Mom.

"Show me." Mom seemed confused when we opened the refrigerator. Her eyebrows raised when she saw. "That's my jar of chicken fat". She never hesitated as she quickly added, "But, I'm sure the cake will be fine".

I was worried. Had I wasted ingredients by adding chicken fat to our cake? Unconcerned, Mom whipped some frosting and put the cake together. In the end the cake was fluffy and sweet with a hint of chicken broth combined with the vanilla flavoring. I was teased, but we ate it all.

We had our own little apple orchard by the old house at the lower farm and another in the pig pasture. Our apples were small and did not have a nice smooth surface like the ones Mom bought from Ski-Hi Orchard, near Devil's Lake south of Baraboo, or from Maple Hill Orchard, a short trip from the village close to the sawmill southwest of North Freedom. In the fall we enjoyed apple bars, sauce, crisps, cobblers and pies. Apples appeared daily at the bottom of the brown paper lunch sacks we carried to school. Best of all was the apple bread Mom had ready when we walked in the back door after classes: bread buttered on both sides, covered with fresh apple slices and seasoned with sugar and cinnamon, then baked just until the apples were pleasingly soft and fully flavored. We wolfed it down while it was still hot before changing clothes and going out for farm chores.

We had two large strawberry fields, one in the garden south of the house and one in the first corner of the half mile road. Mom used strawberries for making jam, preparing fresh strawberry pies and serving as a summer dessert. When we had more berries than we could use, Mom sold them to folks uptown for a quarter a quart. Picking strawberries took hours and was conducted daily over a three-week period in June. Boredom, sunburn and mosquitoes were hazards when picking. One sunny warm day at the beginning of strawberry season, I grabbed shorts and a shirt from the previous year. I had grown and the top of the shorts and the bottom of the shirt did not quite meet. This exposed about three inches of bare skin across my back at my waist as I knelt to pick berries.

"Ow! Owie!" I hollered when I leaned against a chair that evening. Mom looked and saw a nasty red burn across my back. She treated my sunburn with cold cloths soaked with diluted vinegar water. The burn hurt and it peeled, but it never blistered.

We canned vegetables from our gardens: green beans and peas, pickled beets and spiced sauerkraut, corn and tomatoes. Many of the tomatoes were canned as homemade soup or Dad's favorite, tomato juice. We canned seasonal fruits: applesauce and cherries, peaches and pears. We canned jams and jellies of all types: grape and strawberry, gooseberry and elderberry, strawberry and raspberry, blackberry and crab apple. We canned dill pickles and sweet pickles, watermelon pickles and bread and butter pickles. We had three huge gardens if we counted the one by Grandma and Grandpa's house on the lower farm. Our kitchen became an assembly line between Mom, Allen and me. Although David occasionally helped in the small kitchen, he usually worked outside.

Between early hay crops, Mom and Dad worked at St. Mary's Canning Factory on the other side of the village, north of the tracks. They occasionally brought home fresh peas on the vine. Sometimes a hunk of pea vines fell onto Walnut Street in front of our house as wagons rounded the corner hauling the crop from fields to the factory. We kids dragged those vines off the street to the back yard where we shucked and ate them fresh. No one can count the number of hours we picked, washed, peeled, shucked, cut, parboiled, drained or blanched our various harvests.

Dirty water with residual waste of skins, pits and stems from canning was carried to the stockyard by the little barn and dumped over the fence. It could not go down the drain into the septic tank and there was no village garbage collection. The only other option to dispose of waste was to transport it to the dump outside of town. The dump was only open on certain days during the month.

One late afternoon, after we finished canning 40 quarts of tomatoes we had picked early that morning, I was carrying the last awkward dishpan of waste out of the kitchen. I precariously balanced it as I struggled with the metal push latch to open the porch door. "Ouch! Scream! Yowl! Screech!" I had stepped square in the middle of a farm cat lounging in the fading sun on the top step of warm cement. I did not see her because the pan blocked my view when I stepped from the porch. She bit me, three hard bites. The pan of waste and water flew straight up and came down all over me. I was a sorry sight. Mom was concerned, not about me being covered in yuk, but about the bites.

"What do you think?" she asked Dad. "Cat bites can be dangerous."

"We know the cat. It doesn't have rabies. She stepped on it." Dad was matter of fact. I took a bath and Mom applied salve to the bites and taped gauze over them. My leg swelled and turned bright red around the wound. It hurt, but I never went to the doctor. The cat survived.

10
Dining Room

The dining room was a series of contradictions. The beautiful, dark wood table and buffet sat on a worn linoleum floor. A console radio was the source of family entertainment as well as farm reports and local and national news. Lastly, there was a combination desk and glass curio cabinet of finished oak. We called it the *tip-down-thing* because a piece of wood flipped from a vertical to a horizontal position on one side to make a desk. Under the desk was a small cupboard we referred to as the cubbyhole.

My little brother Randy used the cubbyhole as a hiding place to think or be alone. He started this practice shortly after he learned to walk. The first time Randy disappeared we were afraid we lost him. That was because he did not respond when his name was called while he was in the cubbyhole. After that, whenever we could not find him, we first checked the cubbyhole. He usually did not want to come out of his special place. If we did not need him, we closed the door and let him think. He was safe, and we knew where he was. In retrospect, we three older children probably overwhelmed the poor little guy and he needed a break from us.

A large, three-foot square register in the floor in the middle of the south end of the dining room provided heat from the coal and wood furnace directly below. The furnace had no fan, therefore it was radiated heat rather than forced air. It was the only source of heat for the house including the two bedrooms upstairs.

Since it was too hot in the summer and too cold in the winter to change clothes in our upstairs bedrooms, my brothers and I took our day clothes off in the dining room and changed into the matching pajamas Grandma Hilda had made. She sewed them out of bleached feed sacks, added colorful custom appliques and designed matching pillowcases for each of us. When David and Allen were little, they called their overalls "ra-alls" because they parked them in a little pile by the radio every night. They made up the word.

We sat in front of the radio and listened to *The Lone Ranger*: "Hi-Ho Silver, Away!" or *Dragnet*: "Ladies and Gentlemen. The story you are about to hear is true. Only the names have been changed to protect the innocent. Just the facts ma'am." I liked to listen to music, especially WLS out of Chicago.

My favorite treat was Saturday nights when I went to Grandma and Grandpa's house on Franklin Street and listened to the *Saturday Night Barn Dance*. I could sing the words to almost every song while Grandma and Grandpa played cards with relatives or friends. As those evenings wore on, I lounged on the short sofa in their little front room and drifted to sleep to the sound of the mantle clock that chimed on the quarter hour.

Mom listened to Chicago Cubs baseball. Most of Wisconsin rooted for the Cubs until the Braves moved to

Milwaukee in 1953. Mom continued to listen to the Cubs. Sports team loyalties do not change easily. Bob Uecker started calling play-by-plays for the Milwaukee Brewers in 1971. Mom liked to listen to Uecker, but she was always partial to the Cubs.

The dining room table collected junk during the week: newspapers, bills, church bulletins, Sunday school lessons and recipes. Homework and music were later added to the heap. On Saturday my brothers and I helped clean the house. This chore was not an option; it was Mom's rule. By noon we had cleared the table and dusted the furniture. Mom did the floors as we moved from room to room. On special Sundays, we had company and ate dinner at the dining room table. Company was usually Dad's relatives from Minnesota or Mom's family from Reedsburg, her hometown 12 miles away. Sometimes company was a visiting pastor. Allen and I set the table after Mom placed a table protection pad and laid a white tablecloth.

Meals we ate at the table were the most memorable times in the dining room. Mom was a superb cook. She made the most of every piece of meat, liberally sprinkling salt and pepper. Butter and cream were added to most dishes, and a spoonful of sugar enhanced the flavor of a big pot of vegetables. She butchered, peeled, cut, browned, fried, boiled, riced or mashed everything to perfection. Her baking was exceptional, again using butter and cream, making her own sour milk and sour cream for special recipes and improvising recipes when she did not have ingredients.

One Thanksgiving Mom made a pumpkin pie without pumpkin or pumpkin pie spice. When she was done, no one knew it was not a pumpkin pie because it tasted that perfect. She made it from a butternut squash and her own special concoction of spices purchased from the Watkins salesman who came to our door. She always doubled the amount of vanilla extract called for in a recipe and never used vanilla flavoring.

Mom beamed when folks complimented her cooking. One Sunday, Dad's brother (our Uncle Martin) and Aunt Martha visited. Martin and his boys, Orville and Donnie, had a beautiful farm in Caledonia, Minnesota. Mom prepared a beef roast. "This must have been a really good cow," Martin exclaimed after several bites. Then again, "What kind of cow is this? It's really good."

Mom sputtered later, "If Martin would have complimented that cow one more time, I would've swatted him. That worn out old milk cow had nothing to do with how good that roast tasted." In truth, Martin complimented Mom's cooking after we told him the roast came from an old milk cow. I think the meat was so tender and tasty that he still was not sure.

Martha, Grandma Hilda's sister, made it clear she did not eat wild meat, especially venison. She knew Dad, and later my brother David, were hunters and she wanted none of it.

Sometimes venison was what Mom had handy and what she prepared. She made it taste like beef and preached, "When venison is butchered immediately and not placed on the warm hood of a car or not hung in a tree when temperatures are above freezing, it doesn't have a gamey flavor." Martha enjoyed a good deal of venison over the years. No one ever told her.

Mom served roasted raccoon like a hot beef sandwich. It is rich, dark-colored meat that looks and tastes like beef. Before she cooked this meat, I watched her cut hard white clumps of fat from the carcass until not a speck remained. Raccoon meat has a tallow taste if the fat is not removed. Martha enjoyed those sandwiches too.

11

Floor Problems

The dining room floor had a problem: it creaked when we walked on it. The sound carried into Mom and Dad's bedroom, immediately south of the dining room. Initially, the creaks were random, but eventually, they never stopped. Then they got louder.

The creaking started after the old furnace in the basement and big register in the dining room were removed and replaced with a forced air furnace and ductwork in the late 1950s. The creaking was caused by the repair of the hole where the big register had been. Dad decided to fix the problem so Mom would quit complaining about it. After he pounded additional wood and nails to reinforce the original patch, the creaking stopped.

The living room also had a floor problem: it started to sag. As in the dining room, the living room's problem was also along the south wall. The sag started when I got my very own bedroom when I was twelve years old. My new bedroom was the little room off the living room. It had been Mom's sewing room and Dad's music room. Mom's sewing machine and fabric were there, along with Dad's guitar and violin, the piano and other sundries too precious to be discarded. Everything was removed when the little room became my bedroom.

The Kingsbury piano, a big upright of dark mahogany, was moved from the south outer wall of the little room into the living room directly over the center of the playroom below. The floor could not handle the weight of the piano. Dad was determined to fix the sag.

Late that summer, in his not-so-spare-time, Dad located a sturdy white oak post. He hauled the heavy, awkward hunk of wood down the steep basement stairs, around the corner at the bottom, across the laundry room and into the middle of the playroom, directly below the sag in the living room floor. He measured, then, using jacks, lifted the ceiling beam, and cut the white oak post to the exact height needed. He hoisted the post into position between the basement floor and the beam, before removing the jack. Voila, no sag! Mom was happy. Dad was proud of himself as he told folks about his handiwork.

That fall around Thanksgiving time, Dad's brother (our Uncle Rudolph) and Aunt Edna from Caledonia, Minnesota, came to visit. It was not long before Dad and Mom started talking about how Dad stopped the creaking of the dining room floor and how he fixed the sag in the living room. Dad was anxious to show Rudolph his accomplishment and invited his brother to the basement.

After serious discussion and inspection, Dad beamed with pride. "This beam is strong. It's not going anywhere." With his arm extended, he leaned heavily on the solid beam which promptly tipped over and crashed onto the cement floor followed by Dad. After much checking of Dad, the post and the ceiling beam, the brothers had a hearty laugh. The wood had apparently expanded from summer humidity before Dad installed it. Dry fall air and heat from the furnace caused the white oak to contract. Dad had not considered the change in moisture and humidity would be dramatic enough to cause a major malfunction in the fit of his reinforcement. Nevertheless, Dad confessed he should have known better than to crow about his work.

A few days later, the beam was lifted into position and shimmed to the appropriate height to prevent the sag. It never moved again.

Carolyn enjoys a snowman in the backyard of the house at the upper farm in 1950.

12

Living Room

The living room above the support post in the basement was nice, but not special. Mom and Dad sat there in the evening after chores. We got a television set when I was nine years old. It arrived about the same time as my little brother, Randy, and was purchased at Vodak's radio, television and repair shop uptown. Harley and Joe Vodak did the installation themselves.

The installation was exciting for two reasons. First, Mom and Dad had not told my brothers and me we were getting a television. Second, it was highly unusual to have someone in the living room other than our relatives. My brothers and I sat side-by-side on the floor watching in great anticipation, not saying a word as Joe did the inside work. Harley did the outside part of the install.

Joe asked, "What grade are you in?"

"Third grade," I replied. My brothers also answered, "Second grade. First grade."

"Who's your teacher?" Joe probably knew the answer, but I think he was trying to put us at ease, and himself as well.

"Mrs. Bloss," I replied. My brothers followed suit each saying, "Miss Brimmer." That was pretty much the extent of Joe's conversation as he concentrated on his work. Mom frowned at us. Later, she explained we had to pay not only for our television, but also for the time the Vodaks spent on the install. Mom did not begrudge the Vodaks their pay, but she also did not want to pay for time wasted by needless talking. The Vodak brothers did service calls for us over the years, but the novelty of their visits never wore off.

We had rabbit ears for an antenna when we first got our television. Our set had three channels: CBS was on VHF, while NBC and ABC were on UHF. UHF was hard to tune in until we got an antenna mounted on the roof. Even with the new antenna, CBS had the clearer picture.

Aunt Alma, Grandma Hilda's half-sister, bought a new television a short time later. Its cabinet was covered with green leatherette, and it received only one channel. She bought the least expensive model not knowing it could get only VHF. We were shocked someone could get only one channel when we got three. My brothers and I felt sorry for Aunt Alma.

Saturday morning cartoons were my favorites: *Mighty Mouse*, *Woody Woodpecker*, and *Heckle and Jeckle*. Weekday mornings we watched *Captain Kangaroo* with Bob Keeshan as the Captain, who was joined by Mr. Green Jeans, Mr. Moose, Grandfather Clock, Mighty Manfred the Wonder Dog, and Tom Terrific. Tom claimed to be the greatest hero ever and said over and over, "I can be what I want to be, a bumblebee or a tree." We could not see that Mr. Green Jeans' overalls were green because our television showed only black and white. It was a bit of a shock when later I finally saw his jeans really were bright green.

Network programming ended at 10 p.m., followed by 15 minutes of news from the Madison stations. News, sports, stock market (farm stock, not Wall Street) and weather were all included in the 15-minute report. Each television day ended with the national anthem.

Mom and Dad were most interested in the weather because it affected farming. Before we got our television, Mom and Dad were usually sound asleep by 10 o'clock in the evening. After we got our television, Mom and Dad stayed up extra late for the weather forecast. Later the Madison stations extended the evening news to a half hour. The weather was always last. Mom and Dad sputtered, "What're they thinking? Ten-thirty at night is too late to stay up even for the weather report." They turned the television off at 10 o'clock after that and never watched the late evening news again, at least not until years later.

Afternoon programs were a half hour mix of jungle stories, *Jungle Jim* and *Sheena Queen of the Jungle*, westerns with Roy Rogers and Dale Evans or Gene Autry and Gabby Hayes, and a few game shows. Later in the day, *Leave It to Beaver*, *Lassie*, *Father Knows Best*, and *I Love Lucy* were some of our favorites.

Aunt Martha, Grandma's sister, asked Mom if I could join her to watch *Learn to Draw* at her house; we did not have television at that time. Martha ordered the special plastic sheet and pen. Mom had to drive to Martha's house in Reedsburg so I could participate. The sheet was placed on her television screen. The pen was used to trace what the man on the program drew. I could remove the sheet and finish the partial picture on my own or wait until the next week and put the plastic sheet on the television screen in the same place to finish the picture with the man's help.

The Red Skelton Show was my favorite. Who could forget Red's characters like Clem Kadiddlehopper, Freddie the Freeloader, or Gertrude and Heathcliffe, the seagulls? Red ended every show with a little wave saying, "Goodnight for now and may God bless." When my brothers and I did skits for relatives, we copied Red Skelton's material. Many years later I enjoyed Johnny Carson hosting the Tonight Show. This is not a surprise because Carson had been a writer for Red Skelton.

Mom liked Art Linkletter's *Kids Say the Darnedest Things*, Jack Bailey's *Queen for a Day*, ukulele player Arthur Godfrey's *Talent Scouts*, and especially Bill Cullen's *The Price is Right* (four contestants were behind a desk and were required to bid in at least five-dollar increments), *Name That Tune*, *I've Got a Secret*, and *To Tell the Truth*. Bill Cullen was Mom's favorite game show host. She was also partial to *What's My Line?*

My brother Allen, years later, married a woman named Barb Stueve. We learned that Barb's mother, Meda Stueve, visited the studio of *Queen for a Day* with relatives from South Dakota during February 1953. One contestant failed to show up so they needed a replacement. People waiting in line were asked what they would request if they were a contestant. Meda said she would ask for a prosthetic leg for her stepfather. She was chosen, and told the story of her stepfather without a lot of emotion, tears, or drama. She won. In addition to the leg, her prizes included a trip to Santa Barbara, a Maytag washing machine, a roaster oven, clothing, a vacuum cleaner, linens, a makeover, and two large wall murals. Meda's husband, Richard, carried the *Los Angeles Times* picture of Meta as *Queen for a Day* in his wallet the rest of his life.

Dad almost always finished chores Saturday nights in time to watch *Have Gun—Will Travel*, starring Richard Boone as Paladin, and *Gunsmoke* with James Arness as Matt

Dillon and Dennis Weaver as Chester Goode. Chester had a limp from an injury during the Civil War. Weaver sometimes forgot to limp and other times he limped on the wrong leg. Dad did not care. He seldom missed *Gunsmoke*.

Before television entered our house, Dad took us to free shows (movies) playing uptown in the open lot between Max Pawlisch's hardware store and Schwartz's grocery store. Mom and Dad said nothing could be built on that lot because there was a septic tank below it. We watched *Ma and Pa Kettle* and *The Little Rascals* before the main feature, often a western. The exciting conclusion of the main feature usually scared me. When that happened, Dad hugged me close. "It's not real, Susie. Hide your eyes." I buried my face in his overalls. Dad called me Susie as long as I can remember.

Things changed for Dad with television. I watched him watching *Have Gun—Will Travel* and *Gunsmoke*. He once caught me watching him. It was then, he smiled slyly and said, "Ya know Susie, they say that's not real." He nodded at the television and snickered. Somehow when the story appeared on television it became more real to Dad. Watching the story in his home made it personal.

Our family Christmas tree was always displayed in the living room. I started helping with decorations when I was about seven years old. Dad selected our tree and set it in the front window in a makeshift stand: a pail of sand. Mom critically eyed the tree for symmetry, before she had Dad strategically rearrange its branches. He cut a branch from the bottom or where it was full. Then he augured a hole into the trunk where the tree was thin and placed the sawed branch into the hole to fill out the tree.

I sang Christmas carols while I decorated: "Jingle Bells," "Oh Come All Ye Faithful," and "Silver Bells." If Dad was in the house, he sang with me. He had sung in the choir at St. John's Lutheran Church in Caledonia, Minnesota, before he and Mom were married and until they moved to North Freedom. He also played piano, violin, acoustical guitar in both steel and acoustical fashion, and his harmonica, even though he never had a music lesson. As a young man, he and some of his brothers and friends had a band.

Allen kept the violin after Dad died. When Allen retired, he passed it along to his daughter, Kali, who is an accomplished violinist. It is displayed in her home because it is too fragile to be restored. I have Dad's guitar.

After we got a new couch, the Christmas tree went from the front window to the wall between the door and window on the north side of the living room. From then on, the tree was placed on a round wooden cheese crate wrapped in Christmas paper. The crate raised the tree high enough for Mom to see television from her chair. Dad tied the tree close to the wall using eyehooks on the door and window frames to prevent it from tipping over and to keep it out of the way.

We never sat on the new couch except when we had company, and then it felt weird. It was positioned so it was hard to see our television screen when sitting on it, thus, its use was discouraged. The couch showed little wear twenty years later. It still looked new when Mom and Dad moved to their retirement house located south of Walnut Street, behind the Methodist church on the street to the park, in the late 1970s.

Mom's hands never stopped. Her fingers flew as she crocheted while sitting in her chair in the living room. She mostly made doilies. The wispy pieces were saturated with a thick starch solution. She laid them on the stretching board, a wide table leaf covered with batting under a clean feed sack, and pulled the doilies symmetrically taunt by placing the first few straight pins. Allen or I finished the pinning under her watchful eye. These stiff doilies were all over the house for decoration and for protecting furniture. Mom took other doilies to Holtzmiller's Five and Dime Store in Reedsburg where they were displayed for sale, high on their top shelves. I was sometimes with her when she stopped by to see what had sold and whether they needed more. The manager handed money to Mom. She kept a record of inventory and sales in a small spiral notebook.

When I was six years old, Mom taught me to crochet simple edgings on white linen handkerchiefs. When I graduated to doilies, I liked a particular pineapple pattern best. I did most of my work with white crochet cotton but was allowed to choose an accent color for trim. I pored over spools of colorful thread stored in the round wooden cheese crates. I liked turquoise best, especially the turquoise with the silver strand twisted through it.

Mom's critical eye guided my work. She had me rip out and repair mistakes. A feeling of pride welled inside the first time I took my stiff starched work to Holtzmiller's. Weeks later, I was even more enthusiastic about crocheting as the manager handed 75 cents to me. I wondered who bought the doily and was quite sure the turquoise trim with the twisted silver thread was a selling point. This was my first real job; I was about 10 years old. I put the coins into a small glass jelly jar when I got home.

A couple days later I took the jar and my bankbook to the North Freedom Bank uptown and handed both over to Mary Moll, the teller. I had already accumulated over 30 dollars of birthday and Christmas money in my bankbook.

Mary's eyebrows raised above her wirerimmed glasses. "That's quite a sum." I smiled my reply not knowing what to say. "How did you come by this money?" I was hoping Mary Moll would ask me that question.

"I crocheted a doily and sold it." I said proudly. Mary made a small humming sound. This kind of questioning was not unusual in our village, especially coming from Mary Moll. She seemed quite inquisitive about other people's money. She took my coins and wrote the amount into my book, adding it to the total. I was proud of that entry and looked at it every week or so, remembering the good feeling of accomplishment.

Other children in North Freedom also had dealings with Mary Moll. My classmate, Carolyn Myers, had a younger brother John who told me he approached their father, the postmaster, about starting a lawn mowing business in the 1960s. Mr. Myers proposed that John could use the family lawn mower, but John would be responsible to pay for the gas used to mow his customer's lawns.

John made a business plan and decided to charge his customers 25 cents a week. One of John's customers was Mary Moll. Mary's lovely home was on a large lot close to the river on Maple Street. Mary often mentioned to others in the village what a good job Johnny Myers did mowing her lawn.

One year was exceptionally wet and the grass on Mary's lawn grew like crazy. It grew so fast that John had to mow it twice, sometimes three times, a week to keep it looking the way Mary wanted it. This, of course, raised John's expenses because the extra mowing used more gas. Additionally, the price of gas had slightly increased that year. John was barely breaking even. Plus, he was tired from the extra work.

Frustrated, John approached his father and asked him to help out by covering the cost of the extra gas. John did not want to lose one of his best customers. Mr. Myers did not think it made good business sense to support his son in this manner. Mr. Myers suggested that John should tell Mary Moll that he would need to raise the price of mowing her lawn based on how many times a week the grass needed cutting.

John was more than a little uncomfortable with his father's suggestion. The whole village knew Mary Moll watched her money like Scrooge and bordered on being stingy. John said he practiced how to approach Mary, but it took weeks before he found the courage to knock on her front door. He said his heart was pounding and his knees were knocking as he waited for the door to open.

When he explained to Mary he needed to charge her more because of the extra mowing, Mary drew back and loudly sucked in her breath. John was quite sure he was the first person ever to tell Mary Moll she would need to pay extra money for anything. However, in the end, Mary ponied up the extra cash and John continued to mow her lawn.

Top: Harold Schroeder plays his violin while his friend, Elmer Koenig, plays guitar. *Bottom*: Harold plays his violin while his brother, Rudolph, plays banjo. As a young man, Harold and some of his brothers and friends had a band.

13

Mom and Dad's Bedroom and the Cedar Chest

Mom and Dad's bedroom was south of the dining room and held their bed, two small nightstands, a mirrored dresser, a chest of drawers and Mom's Blue Bird cedar chest. The only closet in the house was in Mom and Dad's bedroom under the narrow steps that went upstairs. It was tiny. There were double windows overlooking the lawn and field to the south. Two large elm trees provided cooling shade during summer.

Three other elm trees with bridal wreath bushes between them lined the half mile road providing a privacy hedge along our small front lawn. Mom and Dad collected long stems of bridal wreath from these bushes to put on graves at the cemetery for Memorial Day.

My brother Allen told me he once heard Mom and Dad talk about taking flowers to a special grave in Oak Hill Cemetery on the north side of the village. Sometime later, Mom sent Allen upstairs in the garage to get something out of her cedar chest. It had been relocated from their bedroom to make room for Mom's new Necchi sewing machine. Allen saw some papers that had apparently slipped out of an envelope when the cedar chest was moved. They contained the obituary of a man named Harry Phippen.

This newspaper clipping said Harry died during surgery to remove his appendix; it unexpectedly burst. It also said Harry was Mom's fiancé—before she met Dad. Allen and I learned later Mom and Dad continued to remember Harry with flowers for years.

Mom graduated from North Freedom High School in 1943, a year before Harry died. Mom and Dad married on March 29, 1946, Dad's birthday. Mom was 21 years old; Dad was 34. They moved to Caledonia, Minnesota, where Dad was managing the Schroeder family farm for his mother, my grandma Wilhelmine "Minnie" (Tewes) Schroeder.

I was born in May of 1947. In 1948, Mom was pregnant with my brother David when Dad got sick. He had an appendicitis attack. Mom could not have been prepared for this. It had to be traumatic for her since Harry had died as a result of an appendicitis attack in the all-too-recent past. She was away from her family; she had only her baby girl, and she was pregnant. As she sat in the hospital waiting room, the expected time to complete the surgery came and went, and several extra hours passed. In the end, Dad was okay. The doctor found adhesions in Dad's abdomen requiring additional surgery. It was also around this time Grandma Minnie passed away.

There was never a specific reason given why Mom and Dad decided to move from Caledonia to North Freedom after David was born. What we know is this: after Mom and Dad married, Dad felt he should stay on the Schroeder family farm in Minnesota with his mother because she was suffering from later stage colon cancer and needed care.

Dad's father, my Grandpa Herman Schroeder, married Grandma Minnie, on March 20, 1908. They had four sons, in addition to Grandpa's seven sons from his first marriage.

Dad was the second youngest. Grandpa Schroeder died on July 28, 1917. Dad was five years old.

Grandpa Schroeder's will stated that when a son reached the age of 21, he could either remain on the farm and receive a share of it, or he could receive $2,000.00 and leave the farm.

Walter was 22 years old and Lou was 20 when their father died. The rest of the boys were younger. Whether Walter received $2,000.00 is not known.

The will further stated that the farm could not be mortgaged. A second piece of land, known as the Koch farm, did not fall under that stipulation.

Grandpa Schroeder obviously never considered the Great Depression would happen. However, the Depression did happen. The older boys, Grandma Minnie's stepsons, chose to leave the farm. Therefore, Grandma Minnie had to come up with $2,000.00 every year or so to give them, in addition to making a living for herself and the remaining boys. This put a great burden on her. Grandma Minnie was able to carry out the terms of the will by mortgaging the Koch farm to the hilt. Of course, that meant making the mortgage payments as well.

Dad was the only son who stayed on the farm. He was 34 when he and Mom married. He could have taken his $2,000.00 and left, like his 10 brothers. Minnie could have sold the farm at any time; it was financially solvent. However, Dad's leaving would have forced the issue when his mother was the most vulnerable. She could not work it alone. This was, also, one of the reasons Dad married so late; he felt compelled to take care of his mother. After Minnie died, Dad no longer felt the same compulsion to stay on the farm.

Back in North Freedom, Grandpa Louie had purchased the upper farm in 1943 increasing his work load even as he was getting older. This farm included a second house sitting empty. Grandpa presumably bought the upper farm for Harry and Mom.

Dad likely felt it would be good for Mom to be by her parents in their later years, just as he had been with his mother. Also, David and I were the only grandchildren Grandma Hilda and Grandpa Louie had.

Dad's brother, my Uncle Rudolph, was interested in taking over the Schroeder family farm in Caledonia when Minnie died. Rudolph and Edna raised their four children on the Schroeder farm. Their son, John, eventually took it over from Rudolph.

It was amazing what a flood of thought came from a newspaper clipping that was found in Mom's cedar chest.

Grandma Wilhelmine "Minnie" (Tewes) Schroeder, feeding her chickens on her farm in Caledonia, Minnesota, about 1947.

14

My Bedrooms

Steep stairs led from the living room to two bedrooms on the second floor. At the top step you were already in the first bedroom. It was mine until I was 12 years old. There was no railing around the top of the stairs; you just arrived. A large wooden wardrobe and steamer trunks blocked the gaping hole to prevent anyone from falling into the stairwell.

There were two windows in my room, one to the west and one to the south. From late spring until fall, branches of the tall elm trees waved pointed oblong leaves at me as I looked out of my bedroom windows. In fall, the leaves turned from green to golden yellow before carpeting the yard. Directly below my west window was a tall narrow lilac bush. It provided a bit of shade from a low setting sun for the living room window below. I had to lean close to the screen to see the top of the lilac bush from my room, but in late spring the scent of lilac blossoms floated through my window for weeks.

The elm trees in our backyard shaded my room during summer days and rustled their leaves in the evening, ushering in a lovely coolness. When stifling quiet heat lingered into the evening, I pulled my heavy three-quarter sized bed with its high oak headboard directly in front of the south window to catch a breath of air.

In winter I kept my bed away from those frosty ice covered windows. It was then my brothers and I ran upstairs, dived into cold sheets and wiggled around to warm the bedding with heat from our bodies. Mom and Dad followed us up the steps and listened to our evening prayers. Grandma Hilda sewed my winter sheets of green flannel. When frigid cold penetrated deep through the flannel, Dad held my feet in his warm hands that felt rough and scratchy against my skin because of the heavy outdoor work he did. "I think your feet are warm enough," he would say.

"No, no, no, Daddy." I wanted him to stay longer because this was our time to talk. He left the door at the bottom of the stairs open when he finally departed. It was the only way heat could get to my brothers and me.

A door on the north side of my room led into David and Allen's bedroom. There was neither hall nor private entrance. The boys had to go through my room to get to theirs. They were lucky to have new twin beds with metal headboards that looked like birch wood. Their room, like mine, had two windows. One was to the west; the other to the north. During winter the only heat in their room came from downstairs through my bedroom making their room colder than mine, even though the door between us was always open. They also missed much of the cool southwesterly evening breeze during warm summer nights.

Mom and Dad must have decided I needed my own room with privacy sometime after Randy was born; I was nine years old when he arrived. Initially, his crib was downstairs by Mom and Dad, but with time Randy could be moved upstairs with David and Allen. While they worked to convert the little music and sewing room into my new bedroom, Randy outgrew the crib, and for a time he slept with me. He was no bother. Due to his chronic ear infections, he usually slept upright, slumped over in a sitting position, so he did not take up much room in my bed. He cried if he laid down for very long.

Randy was healthier after his tonsils and adenoids were removed. He required less care once he felt better. He sat in the little stroller cart wearing his red knit woolen hat with the brim and ear coverings as I pushed it uptown to collect the mail. The hat tied under his chin and caused his blond curls to spill onto his forehead. Randy was adamant about wearing the hat when he was outside because his ears hurt if exposed to cold or wind.

I sometimes missed talking with my brothers in the evening after the move, but mostly I was grateful to have my own room. In fact, I was so excited about my new room I forgot all about the green flannel sheets until they reappeared years later as two twisted stitched rag rugs, a gift from Grandma Hilda at a special wedding shower held in my honor.

One thing that warmed us on a cold winter night was when Dad made what he called a "hot one." He made them when one of us had a sore throat or a cold. Even though only one of us needed the remedy, we all wanted one. A hot one was quite warm water with a tad of peppermint schnapps in it. It warmed us, cleared our sinuses and put us to sleep. It likely had no more alcohol in it than does a teaspoon of cough syrup. It was our favorite home remedy.

Randy Schroeder sitting in a stroller cart, 1957. The south side of the family's home is on the right.

15

Our Yard

A grassy lawn wrapped around the west and south sides of our house. Elm trees swayed over two swings, the clotheslines and a sandbox in the backyard. I had a little gray wooden stool to sit on when I first played in the sand. I think Mom had someone cobble it together so my diapers and rubber pants would not get full of gritty dirt. It was raw wood, not sanded or painted, and slivers occasionally poked the backs of my legs and my hands as the wood weathered.

Dad removed slivers with a tweezers and needle; Mom was not good at anything medical. She could put Mercurochrome on small injuries and Bactine on mosquito bites, but that was her limit. Blood made her woozy.

Initially there was a short cement walk extending about ten feet from the back porch toward the gravel turn-around area where we parked our cars. It ended abruptly with a 20-inch drop off. A narrow long cement sidewalk replaced it when the double garage was built in the early 1950s. The new walk sloped south from the back porch, past the new building and stopped at the upper garden, except for a short extension to the southwest exterior garage door. A large patch of rhubarb grew on the south side of the garage.

The stalks were made into sauce, crisps, tortes, and pies in the spring.

We had a push reel lawn mower. Many times, I mowed the entire yard myself, both by the house and by the barn. It took most of a day, but looked beautiful when I finished. Chores or field work took precedence over mowing, so the entire lawn was seldom mowed in one day. I was in the upper grades at school when we got a gas-powered lawn mower.

Moles burrowed in the yard, and my feet often squished into their paths. David and Allen set mole traps along these paths, and as moles burrowed along—"Snap!"—my brothers had them. They saved the little front mole feet and took them to Max Pawlisch's hardware store uptown to collect the reward he paid. Max looked a lot like his brother, Ben, who lived by us on Walnut Street.

"Hello there boys. What've you got for me today?" Max greeted my brothers, already knowing the reason for their visit. My brothers did not look at Max. Rather, their eyes were on the display of fishing supplies conveniently placed at eyelevel.

"Here you go," Max said while handing over the reward money.

The boys continued to peruse the treasures in front of them. Max was purposely quiet letting David and Allen have a good look. "Is there something special you young men are looking for?"

My brothers invariably bought fishing hooks, sinkers and bobbers from Max, as well as .22 shells. Thus, their reward money went back into Max's cash register.

Before Max, Ted Wiegand paid a 10-cent bounty for a pair of mole feet. Old Ted owned the blacksmith shop uptown. States and counties started offering bounties on various ground burrowing rodents in the early 1900s because the holes and tunnels the animals created caused soil erosion. Some Wisconsin townships continued to pay bounties as recently as 2013. Ted Wiegand also sold hunting licenses out of his blacksmith shop, although he had to leave his shop and go to his home to have his wife make out the paperwork. It could be assumed that Mr. Wiegand was unable to read or write, but that was never confirmed.

Ted opened the blacksmith shop when he and his wife, Ida, moved to North Freedom after they lost their property along the Wisconsin River in 1942. The government took their land to build Badger Ordinance Works, later known as the Badger Army Ammunition Plant.

There was a small sandy flower garden with violets, iris, tulips and gladiolas on the north side of the upper yard between the new double corncrib and the house. This crib replaced a ramshackle shed that housed the old farm truck, so it was built double to accommodate housing the truck in the covered area between the cribs.

Mom planted a small patch of asparagus on the west end of this narrow garden. She was excited when several years later, she finally saw spears poking out of the soil. I was sent out every few days with a sharp paring knife to cut asparagus stalks by slicing at an angle just below the ground. Mom lightly boiled the cut stalks, drained the water and served them with butter and salt and pepper. Sometimes she served asparagus with cream sauce, but I preferred it plain. By the time one bunch of stalks disappeared as tasty side dishes, new tender stalks sprang up where I made the initial cuts. This continued for about a month before the asparagus plants went to seed to rejuvenate for the following year.

Our swimming pool sat on the grassy lawn stretching east of the garage. The lawn extended beyond the pool past the south side of the barn, tool shed, rabbit hutch and outhouse. Our swimming pool was actually an old metal cow tank Dad filled with cold water during warm weather. We put on shorts and played in it until we turned blue. Water was held in the tank several days and warmed nicely for our play until a thin scum developed, and the tank had to be drained.

When we were older, Mom took us to swimming lessons twice a week at the public pool in Reedsburg. Lessons were in June, early in the morning. This pool was not heated so the water was icy cold. Our lessons fell in different time slots making it uncomfortable to wait for each other as we started or finished swimming. Blue lips pursed over chattering teeth as we climbed into the car for the ride home.

The drive to and from Reedsburg took us through Rock Springs, a village smaller than North Freedom. It was first named Ableman after the man who settled there in 1851. The Sauk County Historical Society tells us, "Ableman became Rock Springs in 1875, alluding to the many natural artesian springs which abound in and around the village. The name reverted to Ableman in 1879, and in 1947, it again, and permanently, became Rock Springs."

Many folks continued to call it Ableman in the 1950s, likely thinking the name would revert yet again, or maybe resisting the change altogether. It was known for the tall cliffs of quartzite rock surrounding the Upper Narrows on the north side of the village. The quartzite was mined by a business that used dynamite to separate rock from the cliffs. Huge blasts shook the ground and rattled windows in the village daily. Part of the road we traveled for swim lessons ran along the Baraboo River where it flowed through the Upper Narrows and along the quarry.

   Traffic was stopped, and everyone had to exit their vehicles and walk a couple hundred yards to the old stone foundation that served as a shelter from falling rocks during blasting. I covered my ears and bowed my head in anticipation of the thunderous booms that jarred your very soul. We swatted mosquitoes as we waited for the call all was clear to resume our travel. Sometimes blasting made us late for swim lessons.

   On rare occasions, we were treated to an afternoon at the Reedsburg pool in late summer when the water was warmer. We were sunburned and our feet shredded from the rough cement on the bottom of the pool by the end of our play. When we were older, Dad took us to the Quarry Pond or Mill Pond to swim because Mom did not always have time for the drive to Reedsburg. I swam across the Baraboo River several times. I did not like swimming in the ponds or the river because they were brown with mud and I remembered catching huge carp and turtles out of that water. I also saw snakes.

Top: Carolyn sitting on her little stool by the sandbox in the backyard of the upper farm shortly after the family moved to North Freedom, 1948. *Bottom*: L to R: Randy, Allen, David, and Carolyn enjoy a cool dip in the cow tank swimming pool.

Top: Carolyn using a small metal rake in the backyard of the upper farm shortly after the two-car garage (on the left) was built. *Bottom*: Carolyn standing in the lower part of the backyard at the upper farm between a field of alfalfa and the silo. The trees on the left stand along the half mile road. The low line of trees in the far background on the right are in the upper pasture along the Baraboo River.

Pearl and Harold Schroeder standing in the turnaround yard that anchored the upper farm buildings on their wedding day, also Harold's birthday, March 29, 1946.

The Lower Farm

16

The House

Grandma Hilda and Grandpa Louie Kaun lived in the house on the lower farm when our family moved to North Freedom in 1948. We entered the house through the old summer kitchen, not the front door. Many old houses had summer kitchens. They were built that way so the heat of wood stoves used for cooking would not unduly overheat other rooms.

Some of my earliest memories are of Dad or Grandpa carrying me across the summer kitchen because some of the floor boards on the far north side were rotting and not safe. You had to know where to step or you might fall into the crawl space before you reached the backdoor. Later, I knew how to maneuver the summer kitchen myself. The steps into the kitchen were fine.

When I stayed overnight with Grandma and Grandpa as a treat, I slept in one of the creaky metal beds in an upstairs bedroom. The mantle clock chimed on the quarter hour, a soft soothing sound that was my final memory before sleep. The clock was a wedding gift to my grandparents from Grandpa's brother, Albert, and his wife Hulda. It currently graces our home.

I can still see Grandma in her housedress and apron working in the kitchen of their neat and orderly home on the lower farm, preparing meals or baking cookies. I was four years old when I watched Grandma take her good goblets from the built-in cupboard and wrap them in brown tissue paper. She was preparing for their move from the farm to their home on Franklin Street in the village.

After they moved, and when I was in grade school, I occasionally walked through the old house. Several glasses sat in the kitchen cupboard; water still ran in the house. Several framed pictures hung on the walls, portraits of people I did not know. I sat on the sagging mattress of the metal bed in the upstairs bedroom. It brought back eerie, but not scary, memories of Grandma and Grandpa living there.

The bathroom was an outhouse to the east. It was necessary to walk around and behind the wood shed and down the hill toward the creek to get to it. The top of the outhouse was almost level with the summer kitchen so its associated aroma was usually not noticed because the house and farm buildings were on higher ground, and the wind was usually from the west. However, the smell behind and below the outhouse toward the creek was strong, especially on warm summer days.

Our family figured a good windstorm would knock the old house over one day after Grandma and Grandpa moved out, but that never happened. My brother David told me about how the old house came down some 60 years later. When the new owners decided to demolish it, supports of the structure were weakened to make it fall, but that did not happen either. The old house had to be pulled over and actually stayed intact on its side before it was disassembled.

Pearl Kaun and her dog, Sandy, standing in front of the old house on the lower farm. The picture was taken when Pearl was confirmed at St. Paul's Lutheran Church, 1939.

Pearl Kaun and her dog, Sandy, at the north door of the old farm house at the lower farm. A vegetable garden was outside this door. A raspberry patch and a fence loaded with grapevines was beyond the garden.

17

Grandpa and the Church

Grandma Hilda and Grandpa Louie bought the lower farm and moved to North Freedom in 1930. They joined St. Paul's Lutheran Church where Pastor Gustov Vater was serving. Pastor Vater, age 53, his wife, Emma, 43, and their three sons, Christian, age 18, Gerhard "Gay," age 16, and Victor, age 14, had arrived in the village two years earlier.

Grandma and Grandpa were members of St. Paul's for only a few years, five at most. It was long enough for Grandpa to become treasurer of the congregation.

Grandpa's faith was strong, but he had disagreements with the little Lutheran church. One of these was about the pastor's salary during the Great Depression. It upset Grandpa that the church did not have enough offerings to pay Vater's salary, meager though it was, and that the Ladies' Aid had more than enough from their chicken suppers to make up the difference. However, the Ladies' Aid would not part with their funds to help pay Vater's salary. The pastor was often paid with chickens, sausages, vegetables and fruit, but that was hardly enough to feed a family of five.

Grandpa recognized the ladies' good work, but on the other hand, felt the Ladies' Aid money should first be used to help the church meet the pastor's salary, especially under the financial strain of the Great Depression. I am sure the ladies had a valid reason for their decision, but I only heard Grandpa's side of the story.

Grandpa got ornery when someone did not agree with him, and he tended to hold a grudge. Eventually, disagreements between him and the church became too much, and Grandpa and Grandma left St. Paul's and rejoined St. John's Lutheran Church in Reedsburg where they had been members before moving to North Freedom.

Grandma and Grandpa felt sorry for the Vaters. Pastor Vater was doing his work and not getting paid even though the money was there, albeit most was in the Ladies' Aid treasury. His wife Emma shouldered the care of her family under difficult circumstances. Grandma and Grandpa were sure there were many nights when she had to tell her husband and her three boys, in their late teens and early twenties, there was not a lot of food. She likely had no one to share her burdens with—that would be the talk of the town.

Pastor Vater left St. Paul's in 1942. Emma, his wife, died a year later. Mom said, the fact that Emma died a year after leaving North Freedom, at age 57, may have indicated how rough her life had been.

It was to our benefit that Grandma and Grandpa came back to St. Paul's for occasional weekly services and special events, like our Christmas programs and confirmations. It was during these times Grandpa sat stiff in a pew next to Grandma with his arms folded across his chest and a gruff look on his face.

From early on, Gay stayed on the farm when money and food were short at home. Grandma and Grandpa were happy to provide accommodations and meals for Gay. In fact, even after Grandpa and Grandma left St. Paul's, they welcomed Gay to the farm where he often stayed overnight. He would come and go without invitation. Grandpa found extra farm work for Gay to do in return.

Gay and Grandma worked at the Reedsburg Woolen Mill during the Great Depression. During the week they stayed with Grandma's sister, Martha, and her husband, Louie Janzen, and their son Eber, at the Janzen home on North Walnut Street in Reedsburg. Mom said Grandma worked at the woolen mill to keep the farm from being lost to the bank.

Gay eventually scraped together enough cash to buy an old car and drove Grandma back and forth between Reedsburg and North Freedom on weekends unless it rained. Gay's car had a soft top and leaked like a sieve. When it was raining, the Janzens brought Gay and Grandma home for their weekend stay. Grandpa took them back to Reedsburg on Sunday evenings.

Louie Janzen and the boys eventually soldered a sheet of tin on the roof of Gay's old car while it was parked in Janzen's garage. Their garage was a converted chicken coop fixed up with a bit of plaster on the ceiling and walls. When the men put the new roof on Gay's car, they set the soldering iron on top of the car. It left burn marks on the plaster of the garage ceiling that remained for years.

Gay and his wife Erna were friends of my parents throughout their lifetimes. Later, their children, Fred and Louise, were our classmates and friends. We entertained each other while our parents played cards in Vaters' home above their locker plant business uptown.

18

The Pig Barn

There was a lot more in the pig barn than pigs. It was a three-story building built into the hill between the milk house and the creek. The creek was fed by an artesian well and water that drained from higher cropland. The two lower stories of the pig barn could both be accessed at ground level. Grandpa Louie bought the lower farm and moved to North Freedom in 1930, right at the beginning of the Great Depression. Mom, born in 1925, was just a child. The pig barn was built in the mid to late 1930s. Part of the second level served as a garage. During the 1950s, Dad occasionally used that spot to rescue a box wagon of oats or corn from a quick rainstorm.

The floor of the second level was thick with dust and not strong enough to hold heavy machinery, but it stored many of the necessary small items needed during the year. There were hooks holding ropes, the hayfork, pulleys, belts of all lengths and widths, tarps and other tools. There was a grinding wheel used to sharpen tools and field equipment, but it was a toy when I sat on the seat and pumped the pedals listening to the hum of the spinning wheel. The heavy piece of stone took on a life of its own because, when I stopped pumping, the wheel continued to spin for many minutes.

We could look between the floorboards in some places of this second level and see our pigs meandering around in the level below, and we could smell them too. There was a wood-fired cooker in the lower level of the pig barn to keep the pigs warm in cold weather. It was made of a three-foot-wide piece of sheet metal welded in a ring for a base, with a big cast iron pot that looked like a huge kettle resting on its rim.

The cooker was a blessing for my brothers and me during subzero temperatures when we worked for 15 minutes outside, then warmed up for five by the cooker in the pig barn. Sometimes my brothers opened the door at the base where the fire burned and put their feet close to it. I warmed my hands on the big lid of the pot first, then felt down the side until it became too hot to touch. If the temperature was right, I leaned against the pot first one side then the other to warm myself on cold winter days.

The upper level of the pig barn was the best. Open stairs rounded thick with dust from years of accumulation led to the upper room. There was an old pool table complete with balls, cues and chalk. The corner and side pockets were woven of strips of cut leather held together with rivets. We set pails on cans under pockets that had partially disintegrated from age; they caught pool balls with a clatter.

Mom rarely talked about interacting with friends when she attended North Freedom High School during the early 1940s. However, her eyes twinkled when she told us a group of classmates spent their lunch hour playing pool in the upper room of our pig barn. It was one of the few things she did with friends that she mentioned to us. I do not think she had many such opportunities.

Mom's cousin, Victor Beckman, Rudy and Mandy's son, now in his nineties, recently told me the upper level of the pig barn was a tantalizing place when he visited the farm as a youngster. Victor had little other exposure to farm life. This was due in part to his family living in central Madison, our large capital city. Not only could Victor and his brothers play pool, but Grandpa showed Rudy and the boys the bottle of hooch discretely hidden under an old canvas. Grandpa liberally shared his hooch with the group.

Also, on the upper floor was an old car seat with stiff cushions, a psychiatrist couch covered in maroon threadbare velvet with short curved wooden legs, a Victrola music box in a waist high wooden cabinet and a box of records. I lifted the top of the Victrola to play music, placed a record on the turntable and turned the crank on the side of the wooden box to give the internal workings the needed tension before flipping the switch by the turntable to start its circular motion. The needle had to be placed gingerly on the record or it might create a scratch that would forever cause a skip of the music in that spot. Music played at the appropriate tempo at first, and I pretended I was dancing a waltz or twostep in an imagined ballroom. The music often slowed before the song ended, and I had to crank the Victrola again to speed up the beat. My brother Randy still has the Victrola.

There were crude planks mounted at various levels on the south wall and other freestanding shelves that held books and a small stack of discarded comics. I was introduced to Edgar Allan Poe while sitting on the dusty old car seat reading "The Tell-Tale Heart." Hardly breathing at the end of the story, the pounding of my own heart was eerily noticeable. Could that be possible? At 10 years old, I had never before read such a book. Several minutes passed before the courage to stand found me. Watching over my shoulder, I descended the dusty stairs to the pig smell and scurried out the door to find Dad. "The Raven" was eerie. I remembered that poem much later when two of my youngest daughter's friends from the forensic group read it, alternating with "The Midnight Ride of Paul Revere." They received first place in their competition.

Exploring the upper level of the pig barn was unending because of the many random items stashed in every nook and cranny. There were so many things that sometimes I discovered them more than once because I could not remember them all.

19

The Horseshoe

The Baraboo River formed the south and east boundaries of our farm. It flowed generally east as it passed our property. South of the little pasture and artesian well, it made a sharp bend to the southwest, then to the east, before turning sharply back to the north toward the lower farm, forming a small peninsula. After this first peninsula, the river again flowed directly south to make another wide, larger peninsula forming our lower pasture. It then meandered generally east-northeast toward the railroad tracks.

The small peninsula was referred to as the horseshoe due to its shape and was large enough to raise a field of rotated crops. Land on the horseshoe was fertile but prone to flooding. It was accessed from the half mile road by a path beyond the little pasture, going south between two planted fields, through a wooden gate, down an incline past the artesian well and across the upper pasture. There was a small grove of trees where the pasture ended and the horseshoe began that kept the field hidden from view. After it was planted, we checked it frequently.

One dry hot summer day, David and Allen were sent to check the crop in the horseshoe. Trudging as fast as they could back to the lower farm and wide-eyed, they reported,

"The horseshoe is flooded." This was not expected because there had been little rain. Inspection showed beavers had built a dam downstream, causing the river to back up and the field to go underwater.

Dad and Grandpa readied our rowboat with the five-horse Martin motor and oars and collected some dynamite to blow up the beaver dam. After milking cows and just after sunset, they launched the boat.

The motor was cut well before they reached the dam because visibility was poor; the river looked different from the water now that it was dark. They rowed in lantern light to the beavers' barricade. It was quiet as they worked intently at the unfamiliar task of rigging the dynamite along the dam.

Like a clap of thunder, an explosive CRACK! cut the air, jarring the boat, and the men. Dad and Grandpa grabbed each other in a hefty bear hug thinking the end had come. It had not, but what?

A startled beaver had done a warning slap with its tail right beside the boat. Dad and Grandpa said they did not hurt the beavers, but they "blew that beaver dam all to hell."

Their tale always tickled me because the two men were different in their temperaments. Dad was a hardworking, easy going soul; Grandpa worked hard, but was not easy going and tended to be ornery much of the time. Although I did not see it, I am quite sure that is the closest the two men ever were, in body and in spirit. They celebrated their success with a shared swig of alcohol on the milk house steps. That was also part of their story; although, it was not mentioned when the tale was told around Mom. That swig was either from a hidden bottle of grain alcohol or Grandpa's personal stash of hooch saved for special celebrations—like blowing up a beaver dam.

20

Ice Skating

The river flooded the pasture each spring when the snow and ice melted. Two low areas in the marshy upper pasture, directly south of the upper farm, usually retained water throughout the year and were known as the Schroeder Ponds. They were surrounded by bogs and not easily accessible. The ponds were not desirable in summer because of muck and mosquitoes. When snow came, the bogs proved an obstacle for sledding the slopes from higher fields to these bottomlands. Our sleds zoomed a short distance, hit a frozen bog and we were tossed off with a jolt. However, the ponds were great for ice skating and bonfires during the winter.

I learned to ice skate wearing Mom's skates while Dad was ice fishing at Mirror Lake, about 10 miles north of our farm. A dam that powered Timme's Mill in Lake Delton formed that lake. We took shovels to the lake to clear snow from the ice. Allen and I usually skated. David preferred fishing with Dad, although Dad always had extra poles for Allen and me.

My brothers and I talked about the fun we had skating on our ponds at school. Word spread and soon classmates joined us, including those from the upper grades. Big kids began showing up during the day on weekends to help shovel snow and haul wood. Some of the big boys rolled old tires from

Lankey's Skelly Station to the ponds. A fire was often started in the afternoon with scrap wood my brothers collected throughout the year. Once the flames were well established, a tire was added, assuring a place to warm up for an entire evening and a source of light in winter darkness. Graham crackers, chocolate bars and marshmallows materialized for s'mores, and on rare occasions there were hotdogs. Everyone smelled like burnt rubber in short order, but we did not care; it was the best entertainment ever.

By the time I started high school, I could skate backward and do multiple turns. One crisp cold evening when the ice was exceptionally good, I skated across the pond full speed, stopping with several twirls. Receiving attention, I repeated the stunt several times increasing my speed with confidence. All of a sudden, my foot stopped abruptly. The crack in the ice was not visible; my skate caught and was held tight as my body continued to turn. SNAP! My ankle. Pain brought tears that concerned some of the younger children who unsuccessfully tried to help me, then skated to get David and Allen. The boys dragged me to the fire where we saw the skin above my skate swell like a doughnut around my leg. Assuming the pressure on my foot should be relieved, David carefully undid the laces and pulled on the skate to extract my foot. OUCH!

The unanimous decision was I needed to get home. I could no longer wedge my foot into the skate or my boot because of the swelling and could not put weight on the ankle. Carrying me over the bogs was impossible. I hoisted my butt onto a short sled and with help, painfully maneuvered across the crags and dips of the marsh. Dr. Pearson, our family doctor who still made house calls, said I suffered a bad sprain and stabilized my ankle with an elastic bandage. I missed a full week of classes and returned to school on crutches for several additional weeks.

Harold Schroeder and Carolyn ice fishing on Mirror Lake, 1957.

21

The Ram Water System

We did not have a windmill like other farms. The upper farm was on village water. The most unique thing about our lower farm was the self-sustaining ram water system. It provided water for the house, the milk house, and our animals.

The ram was an efficient Rube Goldberg contraption that operated by the principle of gravity and water flow. It was already there when Grandpa bought the place in 1930 and was located directly east of Grandma and Grandpa's house.

The ram was close to a second artesian well at the upper end of the creek. It was needed to regulate the flow of water from the well to the buildings because the flow of water from the artesian well was too inconsistent to be used directly.

Water from the well flowed from an eight-inch pipe. A smaller pipe was connected to this pipe and to the ram. The flow of water from the well supplemented the perpetual motion of the ram. As water accumulated into the bladder of the ram, the increasing weight activated the release of the water to the buildings. Since the ram and the buildings were relatively at the same level, no lift was required. Excess water from the well, not needed by the ram, flowed directly into the creek.

The entire system operated continually on the flow of water from the well and the principle of gravity. Its soft continuous hmtsh—hmtsh—hmtsh could be heard from the old house and throughout the barnyard, like a heartbeat. On rare occasions it stopped. When that happened, Dad or Grandpa had to walk the plank from the edge of the creek across the bogs to prime it. Long stretches of extremely cold weather could interrupt the rhythm. Also, because the fields around the lower farm drained into the creek, heavy downpours, during especially wet summers, caused the ram to go under water. Sometimes the ram continued to operate through these events; but when it stopped, it had to be primed.

Water constantly flowed to the house, the milk house, the galvanized water tank in the barnyard and the lower level of the pig barn. There were two pipes in the water tank in the milk house. One was at the level of immersed 10-gallon milk cans when only their necks and lids showed above the water. The other pipe was offset a little higher as an overflow. The water level in this cooling tank changed frequently during the day, first as heavy cans of milk were plunged in to preserve the milk, until they were later retrieved by the milk hauler from the dairy cooperative. When water reached the overflow level, it was automatically diverted by gravity to the galvanized outdoor drinking tank in the barnyard for the cows. There was a pipe low in the barnyard tank that brought water by gravity to the pig barn.

The water system ended in the lower level of the pig barn with a shut off valve above the large cooker that kept our pigs warm in winter. To prevent flooding the barnyard when water to the pig barn was shut off, an overflow pipe in the galvanized tank in the barnyard diverted excess water back to the creek east of the pig barn.

A gravitational water system in the barn had been designed to provide water to individual watering cups at stanchions for each cow. There was a large water tank suspended above the horse stalls and ground feed boxes in the center of the barn to feed the system. We never used it. It had probably been a well-intended idea, but Dad and Grandpa said it was too much work to maintain compared to its minimum value. Eventually, they removed the tank.

The ram was surrounded by lily pads and watercress when the weather turned warm. Grandma or Grandpa snipped watercress in the spring as long as I could remember. When it became my job, I waved the scissors and small metal pan above my head like weapons to ward off mosquitos as I descended the path to the creek. Tall grass and weeds grew as high as my shoulders, obscuring the slippery sloped path behind the outhouse that led upstream to the ram. The smell of the outhouse settled low into the swale when the air was warm and still. There were spots of slippery green moss on the weathered-gray, sagging plank lying from the edge of the creek to a sturdy low bog close to the ram. I stepped over and around the moss to avoid a slip or fall that might result in a chilly dunk.

Grandma claimed watercress was a delicacy. The first time I tried to eat it I spit it out because of the peppery sharp tang of the leaves on my tongue. Later, I anxiously waited for the unique taste that only happened seasonally.

Historical research indicates the hill to the east and across the creek from the ram was the site of the original Hackett homestead. The site is included on early maps of Sauk County that also show the flow of the Baraboo River changed significantly over the years. Samuel and Dency Hackett, in 1849, were the first settlers in the area that became North Freedom. The village was originally known as Hackett's Corners. It is possible that Samuel and Dency chose this site for their first home because of the naturally flowing water, the creek, and their proximity to the Baraboo River.

My brother Allen's historical paper, "The Old Hackett's Homestead, Where North Freedom, Wisconsin Began" tells us:

> Our grandparents, Louis and Hilda Kaun, purchased their first section of the Hackett homestead in October of 1930. It was most of the original Hackett homestead. They owned the part on which the Hackett log cabin and buildings were physically located. It is the farm at the end of the long gravel road heading south from Walnut Street on the east end of the village. My grandparents would buy almost all the original Hackett homestead by 1943. They, in turn, sold it to my parents, Harold and Pearl (Kaun) Schroeder. My parents bought the first part in 1950 and the rest in 1958. Their youngest son, Randy Schroeder, and his wife Jackie bought it in June of 1980. They sold it in 1982.
>
> The Hacketts settled on the land in 1849. This overview is being written in 2019. Therefore, members of the Hackett Family owned the land or part of it for 52 years. Members of the Kaun/Schroeder family also owned most of the land for 52 years. Together, the Hackett family and the Kaun/Schroeder family owned the land for 104 of the 170 years of the homestead's history.

Crops

Grandpa Louie Kaun sits on the Farmall, model B, tricycle tractor.

22

Hay

Our land along the river was low, prone to flooding and not easily accessible for machinery. This pastureland was where our cows grazed on rich, green grass during the summer. The higher level land to the north was cropland. One crop was hay, either clover or alfalfa, that was harvested and stored to feed our cows during winter. A field could be harvested as many as three times each summer. After cutting, raking into windrows and drying in the field, the loose hay was loaded onto wood racked wagons.

Empty wagons were frequently transported between farms or fields during harvest, along with us kids. We sat on the edge of the floor of these wagons for a bone-jarring ride. Our legs dangled over the side as we gripped a rack, not wanting to get bumped off to a hard landing. We sang at the top of our lungs because the bumpy ride made our voices vibrate: "A Tisket, a Tasket, a Green and Yellow Basket" or "Ta-ra-ra Boom-de-ay." Making up our own silly lyrics added to the fun.

Hay was picked off the ground using one of our tricycle tractors to pull a wagon followed by the hay loader. The tall metal loader had spiky tines rotating on gear-driven chains that picked and lifted windrows of dry hay off the field and dropped it onto the wagon. This train of connected equipment had replaced more labor-intensive methods of harvest years before, but it was nonetheless cumbersome to maneuver.

We had four International Harvester tractors: models C, Super C, M and B. I started driving tractor as soon as my legs were long enough to fully depress the clutch used to put the vehicle into gear and the brake pedal that stopped it. I first watched Grandma Hilda drive while sitting on her lap. When I no longer fit on her lap, I leaned on the tractor fender beside her as she drove. This was good training. I learned it was important to not run over the hay because clover seeds were easily knocked off their stems. These seeds were a nutritious part of the plant. The front tires of our tricycle tractors had to be on one side of the windrow and a large side tire on the other. I quickly mastered negotiating corners to minimize the amount of hay that was run over or missed.

Dad or Grandpa was on the wagon pitching loose hay as it fell from the loader and arranging it to maintain a balanced load. As the wagon filled, the men sunk into the loose hay. I was only nine years old when I started driving this harvest train and soon could not see the person on the wagon from my seat on the tractor. Likewise, the person on the wagon could not see me.

It was easy to miss part of a windrow on a corner. A loud "Whoa" from the person on the wagon was the signal to stop because no hay was coming from the loader. The missed hay was hidden from the tractor driver by the wagon and loader. When part of a windrow was missed, the person on the wagon had to climb down, load that hay with a pitchfork and then climb back onto the wagon.

I drove the tractor slowly to allow the person on the wagon time to move the hay and not be overcome by heat. One warm afternoon in the big field along the railroad tracks, I was driving a long straight stretch going east. In the distance I saw the afternoon mail train approaching the village. As it drew closer, I could not hear the usual deafening sound of the locomotive because the tractor's engine drowned all noise. However, the powerful rumbling of the train traveled along the ground to the tractor seat and steering wheel, rippling through my body. I had never been so close to a moving locomotive before. It was impressive.

"Whoa! Whoa! Whoa!" The shout startled me from my daydream. I had driven toward the train as I was distracted by it, right in the middle of a long straight windrow. By the time Grandpa realized no hay was coming up the loader, I had missed over 30 yards, and Grandpa was not happy. The three-unit procession of tractor, wagon and loader was not easily turned around without causing more problems, including the possibility of tipping over the wagon, the loader, or both. Backing the tractor, wagon and loader was not a good idea because reversing the loader could cause the gears to mess up or break. When I drove back toward the windrow, more hay was missed. Grandpa's look hardened as he climbed off the wagon to pick up the mess I had created. Sweat dripped off his nose and chin as he silently hauled pitchforks full of hay back to the wagon. He did not reprimand me. I learned the lesson myself from that mistake. Pay attention. Never do that again.

Usually, one of our other tractors shuttled an empty wagon to the field and took the wagon full of hay to the barn. Occasionally, the full load was driven directly, but the shuttle process was faster. Such efficiency was important because it maintained the quality of the hay that was critical to milk production. After hay was cut and dried in the field, getting it off the ground and into the barn as soon as possible minimized the moisture it contained. Heavy dew, summer humidity, passing showers and fast-growing weeds could add damaging water or unwanted debris to the crop. Putting wet hay into a barn created mold or worse; it could cause spontaneous combustion.

At the barn, loose hay was lifted off the wagon with a large metal four-tined, clamshell type, fork. The tines operated independently of each other and when separated, had a span of about six feet. A person on the wagon pulled the tines apart and stomped them into the loose hay. A series of pulleys and ropes operated by one of the small tractors lifted the fork full of hay off the wagon and up the outside of the barn to the peak of the roof. Once the fork arrived at the peak, it transferred to a horizontal track that whisked the hay into the barn through the large loft door where it traveled on the track until it hovered above the correct bin. The haymow—"mow" rhymes with "cow"—also known as the hayloft, in the big barn on the lower farm had three bins. Once above the appropriate bin, the fork was tripped with a quick hard tug of the trip rope by a person outside, and the hay dropped.

Someone stood relatively close to the wagon and guided the trip rope as the load of hay ascended to the peak because it was important the trip rope did not get tangled in the pulley system. The tripping mechanism was located on top of the fork, obstructing its view from the person on the wagon who stood aside in case of an accidental trip. If there was no one to watch the trip rope, the person on the wagon climbed down to guide it. The tractor operating the pulley system had to be driven slowly and with some, but not too much, hesitation as the load hit the pulley transferring it from the vertical lift to the horizontal track. A spontaneous trip could happen if this action was performed too fast or jerky.

When the load was above the correct bin, the person in the loft yelled, "Whoa," to signal the person on the wagon to signal the tractor driver to stop. Dad or Grandpa determined which bin was to be filled based on the level of hay in each bin, how the hay packed, and how much moisture it contained. The three bins were kept at about the same level during harvest because that was the easiest way to maneuver between them. It minimized climbing the ladders between the bins.

Hand signals were used outside because the noise of the tractor obscured vocal commands. Once the load was steadied over the appropriate bin, the person in the loft yelled, "Trip it." The person holding the trip rope gave it a good yank causing the loose hay to drop from the fork and signaled the tractor driver to reposition for the next load. Workers in the loft then moved this hay, mowed it, to the sides of the bin with a pitchfork before the next load arrived.

It was important not to drive the tractor after the "Whoa" signal. Once inside the barn, a forkful of hay could be pulled forward into the loft by hand with ropes. It was trickier to move it backward because too much slack in the rope could work the fork off the track. Getting the fork back onto the track meant having to manually adjust the rope and pulley system high in the peak of the barn, a dangerous and time consuming task.

Any abrupt or incorrect movement during this process could accidently trip the fork, causing the load to drop spontaneously. An unplanned drop of a forkful of hay could cause injury to the man outside on the wagon or to the person in the loft.

When I was four years old, I sat on Grandma Hilda's lap as she slowly drove the tractor forward, then backward, operating the pulley system to lift hay from the wagon and maintain tension on the rope as the fork was maneuvered in and out of the barn and lowered for the next load. She asked me to listen for "Whoa" and watch for hand signals. I was to warn her when the tires got close to pulley ropes laying on the ground as she backed the tractor to the initial position because it was important not to run over the ropes or have tractor tires on them as the pulley system operated. The nuances of this task became engrained in me.

It was not until I started driving the little International tractor myself for this task at age 10 that I learned how easy it was to become bored with the tedium. Little by little I came to realize how important the job was. The tractor could be the contributing factor of a spontaneous release of a fork full of hay. Driving at turtle speed both forward and backward was critical. Voice and hand signals were important. Your eyes and ears needed to be constantly attentive. Nevertheless, the person on the wagon stood safely off to the side when the forkful of hay ascended and when the empty heavy metal fork clanked its return down the side of the barn to the wagon.

One day my brothers, David and Allen, were on the gravel driveway that anchored the farmyard between the buildings on the upper farm. Mom was on a wagon of loose hay in front of the little barn and was pulling apart the heavy tines of the awkward fork when she was surprised by something that could have been quite dangerous. My brothers saw her drop the hayfork and make a quick grab. She held a five-foot long snake in her fist. Its tail twisted in the loose hay at her feet. With a mighty stroke, Mom heaved the twisting reptile to the gravel not far from the boys.

"Kill that snake," Mom yelled over the noise of the small tractor. Allen and David looked at each other wide-eyed and confused; they were only eight and nine years old.

"How?" They hollered in unison.

"Step on its head."

Allen stayed away, wanting no part of killing the snake. David slowly and cautiously approached the squirming critter that was obviously stunned by its recent short flight. With a swift move, David picked up the snake by the tail end and threw it into the barnyard. Dad said he took care of the snake, but I am not sure if he did, or only said he did, to ease our minds. If the snake managed to slip away, it probably retreated back to the field it came from, not wanting to be tossed about again. This event was discussed at the supper table and was brought up during other mealtime conversations, including those with our hired men, both for the excitement of the story and to caution everyone that dangers lurk in loose hay.

Mowing hay is a critical job because it is important to appropriately maximize the amount of hay stored for cattle during winter. If forks full of hay are dropped into the loft one on top of the other, the hay packs tightly into a big mound from the force of the drop and weight, making the compressed hay difficult to pull from the bottom of the pile. Additionally, the stack might tip over potentially causing an injury or fatality, or it could block the chute, the narrow access route from the bottom of the loft to its upper regions. Mowing hay to the sides of the loft loosens it and allows drying to continue, minimizing mold and the possibility of spontaneous combustion.

It was a proud day when I was finally sent to the loft to mow hay. I was now 11 years old, strong for my age and could handle a pitchfork. It was late in the harvest season as I climbed the ladder from the barn floor and entered the lower part of the chute where the ladder continued vertically straight up, until I had to transition to another vertical ladder. Our chutes were a series of mismatched ladders and pieces of wood that formed a structurally strong vertical narrow access route to hay at all levels in the loft. I was almost to where the slope of the barn roof began before I arrived at the top of the hay in the middle bin. After tossing many forkfuls, I gingerly stepped down the ladder out of the mow, exhausted, but I smiled when I heard Dad say, "You did good, Susie."

The sun had shifted onto the metal roof on the south side of the barn a week later when I climbed the ladder into the heat of the loft. The novelty of mowing wore off quickly. The first forkful of hay darkened the loft as the load transitioned to the horizontal track. "Whoa," Grandpa Louie yelled as the load approached the middle bin. Stems of dry alfalfa dropped as it swung precariously. "Trip it," Grandpa yelled. Thunk! The hay dropped, and blinding dust arose. Like the men, I wore a handkerchief folded in a triangle to cover my nose and mouth; my curls caught where it tied at the back of my head. Even with this protection, I blew chunks of black snot after a day in the loft. Grandpa and I pitched the load to the sides of the bin as the fork clanked its way across the track, out of the barn and back to the wagon. We had hardly finished mowing the first load, when the next forkful lumbered to the peak of the barn to darken the loft.

"Whoa," Grandpa yelled. The load swung a bit before the fork was tripped. Thunk! This continued over and over until the wagon below was empty.

Someone climbed the ladder with a jug of water while the next wagon of hay was maneuvered into place below the peak of the barn, and then it started all over.

"Susie. Susie? Are you okay?" I remember being so very warm then feeling suddenly cool then cold and shivering with goose bumps. "Can we get her down the chute?" Who was talking; I wondered? "Better to cool her up here with water."

I was deep in suffocating, prickly hot hay; my mind was foggy. Eventually I climbed down the chute on my own with one of the men below me on the ladder and another above. I was not scared, more surprised. I had had too much heat. It was important to maintain communication between workers during warm weather; heat related issues were common in the agricultural community. After my episode in the loft, I realized how dangerous mowing hay could be. It was no longer tedious to drive the tractor operating the pulley system. I knew the people in the mow depended on me.

23

Fall and Winter in the Mow

The success of our harvest was evident when temperatures cooled, pastures froze and winter set in. Large beams divided the three bins in the hayloft of the big barn. Summer hay crops usually filled the loft by fall. I climbed the hay chute ladder from the floor of the barn to the ceiling that was also the floor of the loft. From there auxiliary ladders and beams had to be traversed to the top of the hay in the middle bin. Mowed hay packed tightly on the sides of the chute and minimized the foot and hand holds around the rungs. My fingers wheedled along the edges of the various ladders to secure a firm grip. My toes pushed into the hard-packed hay until my foothold was secure.

  Getting into the bin at the top of the chute was tricky because hay around the top was slippery. To avoid falling down the chute, I climbed past the top of the hay, jumped toward the center of the bin and scrambled away from the precarious opening on my hands and knees. The top of the chute could be a dizzying thirty feet from the barn floor in the fall of the year.

  All three of us kids were needed to toss hay from the loft as temperatures dropped and the food supply from the pasture dwindled. Dad told us from which bin to pull hay for daily feedings. We always started with the middle bin because that is where the chute was. When the level of hay in the middle bin was down about 10 feet, we climbed the wooden ladders built along the heavy beams dividing the loft and pulled hay from the east or west bin into the middle bin. That hay had to be moved twice, first to the middle bin then down the chute. We did this as fast as we could because that gave us more time to play in the loose hay. We dared each other to jump from the high level bins into the hay in a low bin. As we jumped, the hay compacted making for hard landings. If landings became painful, we grabbed our pitchforks and tossed loose hay onto the landing pad, being careful to move our forks to the sides of the loft before we resumed our acrobatics. We usually jumped feet first and sometimes on our butts, bellies or backs. Occasionally, I attempted a somersault.

Hay was tossed with three-tined pitchforks. It was important to toss a forkful that would slide all the way to the barn floor below. The chute widened and narrowed depending on how hay had been mowed and compacted. If a forkful became lodged in the chute, another forkful could be tossed on top in hopes it would knock the first forkful loose. If two forkfuls did not drop, it was necessary to sidle along the side of the barn to the top of the ladder, climb down to where the chute was plugged, then kick and push to force the hay to the floor of the barn. Dad said we should not take our pitchforks to clear the chute like he did because it was dangerous. After clearing the chute, it was necessary to climb back into the loft to finish the task.

When the pile of hay tossed to the barn floor reached the ceiling, it was necessary to climb down the ladder and push the pile of hay away from the chute so it was ready to feed the cows at their stanchions. The amount of hay required depended on the number of animals needing food and the amount of pastureland available for grazing. During winter months when cows could not graze in the pasture, it was necessary to push three or more mountains of hay onto the barn floor. One cow eats a bathtub full of hay each day if she cannot graze in the pasture.

24

Stuck in the Mow

During the winter, my brothers and I had daily chores at both the upper and the lower farms. David and Allen did chores together. I did chores alone because I was bigger and stronger. Dad alternated us between the two places. One November, it was my turn to do chores at the upper farm. Dad and Grandpa were deer hunting 40 miles to the north and would not be back until milking time. It was a big deal for them to hunt up north. With both Dad and Grandpa gone for the day, chores were running behind schedule.

The haymow in the little barn was full of our summer harvest. I cautiously climbed the ladder and hurriedly tossed hay down the chute for the youngstock because it would soon be dark. Knowing this would be a quick job, I had not turned on the light in the loft. There was only one light in the barn loft on the upper place; its switch was in the lower level of the barn. The bulb had a clear glass dome protector and was located high enough so it would never be buried in hay; there was no ladder to it. It burned out often and could not be changed until there was enough hay in the mow to reach the bulb. There was seldom that much hay. Light from the bulb could be seen between the barn boards from the house. Mom frequently checked the loft light, and if she saw it was shining when she knew no one was in the barn, she sent one of us out to turn off the light. It was because of this; I did not turn on the loft light unless it was absolutely necessary.

The shaft of the chute in the small barn had been built in offset sections. This made it difficult to see if the hay I tossed down was actually falling all the way to the barn floor. The youngstock did not require as much food as our milk cows; therefore, I was confident if some hay got stuck, I could force it through the chute.

It was already dusk when I finished in the mow and started down. Against Dad's warnings, I took the pitchfork with me. Stepping into the dark and maneuvering past the first offset, I incrementally stuck the pitchfork into the walls of packed hay around me. Step down—step down. My foot rustled into loose hay as I moved lower. I was about halfway down the chute and waist deep in loose hay when I felt a solid pack. Peering through eerie darkness, my grip tightened on the pitchfork. With one hand firmly on the ladder I awkwardly used the fork to loosen hay on either side of the plug. Satisfied with my effort, I repositioned myself lower on the ladder deep in hay, tightened my grip on the fork and gave a hefty shove directly into the middle of the pack. Nothing. A shove to the left. Nothing. A shove to the right. Still nothing.

Darkness enveloped me. Disoriented from my efforts, I climbed up several rungs to collect myself. I knew Dad would not be happy I was in the hay chute with a pitchfork in the dark, so I used my foot to firmly secure the tines into the solidly packed hay between rungs. I would collect the pitchfork after the chute was open.

I stepped down again as far as possible into the hay. Holding tightly to the ladder, I got into a low squatting position with one foot solid on the plug. With my hands wheedled up and around the back of a rung and my knees bent, I lowered my other foot to the plug and tried to force the hay through the chute by straightening my legs and pushing up with my arms. It was no use. I was stuck in the haymow. Dad and Grandpa were gone. David and Allen were at the lower barn.

I could see nothing in the sinister darkness. What should I do? Do not panic. First, locate my pitchfork. Then get out of the chute. Slowly and carefully feeling my way back up the ladder, I located the pitchfork. It was wedged so tightly into the hay I could not retrieve it until I climbed past it and pulled up. With a tight grip I repositioned the fork higher. I knew a pitchfork could quickly become a dangerous weapon in a hay chute if not handled appropriately. At the top of the chute, I tossed the pitchfork far away from the opening to prevent it sliding back at me. I could see moonlight through the tiny pulley hole in the upper corner of the barn near where the roof began. The only other light was moonbeams between the vertical barn boards of the hayloft.

Would anyone miss me?

Not for awhile.

The temperature was falling fast since the sun had set. I was shivering because I was now wet with perspiration from tossing hay, trying to loosen the plug and climbing the ladder. My cumbersome work coat had been left in the lower level of the barn. I had to let someone know where I was. I had to make some noise. The only thing I could do was holler. Help? It was not in my nature to ask for help. "Maybe I don't need help," I thought. "Well, yes I did."

What was that? Someone or something was in the driveway. What? It was too early for Dad and Grandpa to return from hunting. We seldom had company in the middle of the week and never during chore time. I would not further embarrass myself or Dad by letting company know I was stuck in the mow. I would not holler for help.

Voices! Excited! Dad! Mom! A buck! How many points? Dad had never before shot a buck. I knew he would go uptown for a short celebration. "Dad, don't leave me." I barely breathed the words.

I loped through the loose hay across the loft to the narrow ladder leading to the pulley hole. Hollering was a waste of energy at this point. I scrambled up the ladder toward the moonlight ignoring the fact I did not like heights. It was so dark in the loft I could not see the distance, but I figured the pulley hole was about 10 feet above the soft hay. However, looking through the pulley hole onto the driveway below was a dizzying 30 feet. Oh my, it took my breath away. Light snow was falling and the yard light created a dazzling scene. Elsie and Dan, our neighbors, were looking at the six-point buck. Dad was smiling; I could hear it in his voice.

"Dad?" I croaked. My voice sounded little. Talking below continued.

"Dad," I said it a little louder trying not to sound desperate. Nothing. It was no use. I had to yell. "Dad! Daddy! I'm here!" The talking stopped.

"Dad! Daddy! I'm up here!" I could see the figures below moving around.

"I need help! I'm up here!"

"Susie, is that you? Where are you?"

"I'm up here. I plugged the hay chute. I can't get out."

"Where are you?"

"Up here."
"Are you by the pulley hole?"
"Yes."
"Get down from there. Right now. Go slow. Be careful."

I did exactly as I was told. Tears of relief and humiliation came as the single bulb spread its soft glow through the mow when Dad flipped the switch below me. I stepped down the ladder onto the hay and sat at the top of the chute waiting for him. How could I have done this? Dad was proud of his buck. Now he had to dig me out of the haymow.

A good while later and after a lot of sputtering, I was standing in front of Dad on the barn floor burrowing into my warm coat. "Susie, how did you manage to get that much hay packed that tight?"

"It was getting dark, and I couldn't see it was stuck so I just kept throwing. I took the pitchfork with me to help push it through. I know I am not supposed to, but I was careful. I tried to loosen the sides then pushed with the fork. Then I anchored the pitchfork and climbed into the plugged spot and tried to push it through with my feet. It was really dark." My story was told in a single breath.

Dad shook his head. "Well, Susie, that's the most hay I have ever seen plugged in a chute. Did you learn anything?"

"I won't do that again." My voice was quiet.

"I don't think that will happen again." Dad put his hand on my shoulder and turned me to the door. "Would you like to see my buck?" He sounded happy again.

25

Doctor Pearson

Toward the end of summer when regular pasture grass turned dry and brown, a recently harvested hay field close to the lower barn was used as a temporary pasture. Dad and Grandpa would build an electric fence around one of these fields as needed. An electric fence was one string of barbed wire strung on thin metal posts and charged with electricity using a battery. We dared each other to touch the wire with a weed stem or small branch. This delivered a stinging shock to our fingers. Cows were herded into these makeshift pastures to graze, which allowed our regular pastureland to rejuvenate while our cows chewed on the relatively nutritious stubble of crop left in the field.

Late one afternoon at the end of August when I was six years old, Dad and Grandpa had just finished building an electric fence around the big field adjacent to the garden by the old house on the lower farm. The last of second crop hay was being harvested from the field. David, Allen and I were close to this fence, between Grandma's vegetable garden and the field, picking dark purple grapes and red raspberries as a late afternoon snack. We had walked the narrow dirt paths between rows of vegetables I had helped Grandma weed earlier that week.

The raspberry patch and grapevines along the fence were not weeded. We were shoulder deep in thick summer grass. I was munching on a handful of fruit when I heard the small tractor and looked up to see Grandma hauling the last load of hay from the field to the barn. Dad and Grandpa would herd our cows into that field after milking and connect the fence to the battery.

"Let's go before someone sees us." I was concerned because we had not asked permission to help ourselves to our snack.

"Wait. I want another bunch to take with me." David was grabbing fistfuls of grapes and stuffing them into the pouch he had made by pulling his shirt out in front of him. "Me, too." Allen followed suit. My brothers were always hungry.

Turning from my brothers, I saw something move. Quick as a flash. A smooth, quick flash. I screamed. A snake! By my foot! A long black snake! A long black snake with green stripes! Run, run, run to Grandma!

Bam! Snap! I was on the ground. David, too. And Allen. We were all bleeding. We had hit the recently placed fence, the barbed wire fence.

A barb scraped the top of Allen's head, front to back.

A line across David's forehead dripped red to his nose and cheeks.

I could not see. A barb caught me in the eye.

I was loaded into the car with cloths on my face. Shortly, Dad carried me up the long flight of stairs to Dr. Pearson's office in Baraboo, seven miles from the farm. Mom had made the call from Elsie's house because we did not have a telephone, but she hopped into the car with Dad and me for the short ride to Baraboo.

The doctor had already closed his practice for the day, but agreed to meet us at his office to check my eye. His office was on the second floor of a big brick building behind the bank, on the corner of Oak and Third Street. The windows, tightly closed for the day, held in the intense heat of the sun shining on the bricks outside. It was hotter than a haymow in summer when the doctor ushered us into his examination room and turned on the fan.

Dad held me down on the table while Dr. Pearson cleaned my eye so he could assess the situation. "There does not seem to be injury to the eye itself, but there is significant trauma to the tissue around the eye. I am going to have to close the cuts across her eyelid, her eyebrow and above the bridge of her nose."

Dr. Pearson hummed an unfamiliar tune as his hands worked on my face. Then I heard, "I tried tape to prevent scarring, but there's too much perspiration. The tape does not stick." More humming. "I have some clamps that might work. If not, I'll have to stitch."

None of that sounded good to me. I put up a big fuss, thrashing about and making a lot of noise.

"I have to freeze her eye. You're going to have to hold her really tight, Harold."

Peeking with my good eye, I saw the needle. It was big.

"You know," Dad said, "I don't know if I can take this. I don't feel so good."

"Oh, okay. You look white. Let me take over." Mom never did well with medical things or injuries. However, her concern for Dad did not escape my attention.

Dr. Pearson's finger pointed at me. "You. Lay still." He raised his eyes. "Okay, Pearl, here we go."

North Freedom

I saw the needle coming at me, closed my eyes and screamed. Immediately, there was a heavy sound and movement. Peeking with my good eye, the doctor was pointing at me again. "You. Don't move."

"You got her, Harold? You got her?" Where was Mom? Not by me. Where was Dad? What was going on? Dr. Pearson disappeared.

"Can you hear me? Can you hear me?" Dr. Pearson was talking, but I could not see him. I could hear fine. It was my eye, not my ears. Where was everyone?

Dr. Pearson awkwardly rose above me. "Now lay still. Let's have a look." As the doctor clamped my eye together, Mom laid on the floor moaning. She had passed out as the needle went into my eye. She threw up.

My eye was totally covered with an impressive bandage. Freezing had eliminated the pain. I walked alongside as Dad and Dr. Pearson helped Mom down the long flight of stairs and into the car. She continued moaning as we drove back to North Freedom. After he got Mom home and into bed, Dad took me uptown for ice cream.

I started first grade the following Tuesday, the day after Labor Day. This was my very first day of school; North Freedom did not have kindergarten. A different bandage covered my eye that day. The new bandage hid the clamps in my eyebrow and above the bridge of my nose, but I could peak under the bandage and see my feet with my injured eye.

On the playground, one of the big girls looked at me. "Eew-w. That looks awful." Her friends looked at my eye and ran away. Before recess ended, I went to the girl's bathroom in the basement of the school and inspected my eye in the mirror. There were little crystals of yellowish-brown gunk collecting on the lower part of the bandage. It looked icky.

I did not want anyone to see me, but I had to return to the classroom. I bowed my head the rest of the day.

Mom soaked the bandage with warm Epsom salt water when I got home because it stuck to my skin. The clamps were left uncovered until I went to bed. I told Mom what the big girls said.

"Don't worry about them," she told me. "They're just jealous because you're getting attention."

The bandage Mom applied that night was smaller and my eye did not drip yellow gooey stuff the next day. I had a red line in my eyebrow and a scab above the bridge of my nose for a long time after the clamps were removed. Neither the big girls nor anyone else at school ever talked to me about my eye again.

26
Oats

We raised oats for seed, for feed and for straw bedding for our animals. Rather than buying seed, Dad saved what he considered the best oats and stored them in the granary. He ran those oats through the fan mill before planting them the next season. The mill shook and blew air over the seed grain to remove dust and fine weed seeds. Cloth bags of seed grain were transported to the ends of the field to be planted. Dad harnessed two of our workhorses to the planter, which they pulled to a freshly prepared field. The planter had long narrow wooden boxes where Dad dumped bags of oats seed grain. An auger turned over a gauged slide at the bottom of these boxes to regulate the distribution of the seed.

Alfalfa, or sometimes clover, seed was loaded into separate smaller boxes on the planter and was sown along with the oats. The crops grew together to maximize yield. After the oats were harvested, the grassy alfalfa, or clover, continued to grow above the oats stubble and could be harvested at least once later in the year. The alfalfa or clover remained dormant over winter and became bountiful fields of green to be harvested as hay the following summer.

Alfalfa and clover are legume plants. Legumes add nitrogen, stored in their roots as natural fertilizer, to the soil. After harvesting up to three crops of hay each summer, soil was turned over by plowing. This prepared the nitrogen rich soil for corn planting the following year. Thus, our crops were rotated to maximize yields.

I hopped up beside Dad on the foot stand behind the planter boxes. "Giddap, Giddap," he called to the horses, and away we went at a slow but steady pace. Dad held the reins and directed the team to keep rows straight and close together but not overlapping. He raised the lid of each box to check levels of seed as we progressed and frequently refilled the boxes so no part of the field was left unplanted. He planned stops at the edge of the field where he had staged the extra bags of seed. If a box emptied midfield, Dad had to walk back to the extra bags, hoist one on his shoulder and lug it to the planter.

My job was to watch seeds fall into the ground and be covered with soil. If they stopped falling, it meant the box was empty or the auger had stopped rotating. A stone or stick wedged in the bottom of the box could stop the auger. It was important to know exactly where seeds stopped falling because there would be no crop in that area of the field if seeds were not planted.

After the seeds dropped, they were covered with soil by a series of special harrow discs, circular curved pieces of metal, at the bottom of the planter. These pieces of metal could be bent by a rock or a hard clump of dry soil, or they could break. If seeds were not covered, flocks of birds devoured them, and an entire field of grain could disappear in a day. My eyes shifted between the dropping seeds and the discs while we moved across the field.

It was relatively quiet while I stood next to Dad. The wooden exterior of the planter boxes muffled the soft, smooth sound of the turning auger, hiding a potentially dangerous tool. An auger could promptly amputate fingers or a hand. We seldom spoke, but Dad hummed as he concentrated on the task at hand. The heavy clop of horse hooves on the soft ground and the slicing of soil was a rhythm of soft percussion to his tune. Behind the planter, the tracks of covered seeds were barely visible. In late summer, golden shafts of oats waved from those tracks like a mighty crescendo in a symphony that had begun with Dad's tune.

Harold Schroeder stands behind the oats planter holding the reins of his workhorses. Carolyn often rode on the oats planter with her Dad.

A wagon of oats bundles is waiting to be unloaded into the threshing machine.

27

Harvesting Grain

We first cut oats with a binder pulled by our horses. I was a young child, just old enough to remember, when a tractor replaced the horses. Oats are a fragile crop; nutritional grains are easily knocked from shafts. A large reel softly swept shafts of oats onto a low-slung canvas apron, moving them to a bundler which incrementally bundled the shafts and tied each bundle with a single strand of twine. A fork, comprised of several long prongs, gently dropped these uniform bundles on the ground.

Grandma Hilda rode the binder behind our horses because she best operated the apparatus that knotted the twine. Precise timing of the needle arm and knotting apparatus required constant attention and adjustment. Grandma's nimble fingers, and familiarity with knotting from years of tatting lace, made her best equipped for this task.

Oats were dried in the field by manually assembling individual bundles into shocks. Each shock was two arms full of bundles propped vertically against each other in order to let them air dry. Another two bundles were draped horizontal over the vertical structure to form a protective roof. Water shed off the slippery oat shaft roof, and drying continued even through occasional rain.

Shocks of dried oats were carefully lifted with a pitchfork onto a wagon and slowly transported to the barnyard. Fast, jerky handling of dried oats knocks grains off shafts, reducing crop yield. The twine holding each bundle was cut and removed before the grain was fed into our threshing machine. Twine was removed for two reasons: first, it might tangle and jam the gears of the threshing machine; second, if it made it through the machine and was blown into the straw stack, one of our animals might eat it. Ingested twine could require the help of a veterinarian or worse, cause the death of the animal.

Our threshing machine was a huge gray metal belt-driven box. Bumblebees frequently made their nest inside the machine while it was stored. Dad gingerly moved the threshing machine out of the shed to where the straw pile would be built and carefully put on the belts. Once the belts were assembled, he shouted a warning before the belt drive was engaged. Bumblebees flew everywhere. My brothers and I knew this would happen and did not want to miss the action, but we watched from afar until the bees left, and it was safe to return.

One stifling hot summer day at the upper farm, Dad saw dark ominous clouds accumulating. He was dripping sweat as he rushed to cover wagons loaded with oats. One load was still uncovered when the rain and hail started. He grabbed his old leather jacket hanging on the wall inside the new garage for protection and started toward the exposed oats. As he pushed his arms into the sleeves, he started to scream. I heard him from the porch.

It is a scary thing to hear your Dad scream. I stood there frozen. Mom dropped what she was doing and ran toward him. The bumblebees had built a nest in Dad's jacket. He had stings all over his back. For days I watched squeamishly as Mom applied special cream to the raised red welts. Dad winced at her touch.

The threshing machine operated by a series of belts and gears that required an external source of power. First, we used the old McCormick Deering 1350, the rusty tractor sitting in the old shed on the first corner of our road. It had steel wheels; the back ones were cogged. The cogs made it suitable for plowing soggy fields in the spring. Later we used the McCormick Deering 2236 for power; it was a big red behemoth. Both of these tractors were started with a hand crank and were deafeningly loud. They required patience, time and a lot of adjustments. Both tractors had magnetos, self-generating ignition spark distribution units that were the source of most of the problems. Dad and Grandpa constantly worked with the magnetos and continually vented frustration. Sometimes I thought they were sabotaging each other, but I eventually realized the magnetos were the only problem, not Dad and Grandpa. Despite these problems, both tractors were necessary. They had the drive power for belt driven machines, and they had pulling power for heavy plowing.

Watching Dad assemble belts on machinery was a learning experience. Some went around multiple pulleys and others required a twist; it was like a puzzle. When my brothers were older and strong enough, they helped with the rigging.

Threshing machine belts were not available for purchase. Dad occasionally bought used belts at farm auctions. Some fit our machines; others were shortened or lengthened by splicing to fit. Most of ours had splices and repairs that were done by Dad or Grandpa. Often the widths of spliced sections were different than the original belt; an eight-inch belt might have a five-inch section spliced into it. Some of our belts were more splices than original, a hodgepodge of widths. It did not matter as long as our machinery operated.

Whichever belts were used, they received careful attention. A special dressing was applied to keep them pliable through the 11 months they were not in use. The pleasant fragrance of the dressing floated throughout the year in the second floor of the pig barn where they were stored.

Year after year the threshing machine was set in the same spot. Once the belts, tractor and power drive were balanced, they were not moved until the annual harvest finished. Oats was fed into the machine by laying it on a rotating apron. Dad or Grandpa stood on the edge of the machine or on the wagons to unload the oats.

Straw and chaff blew out of the nozzle at the end of a long extendable blower used to build a large straw stack by the barnyard, so the straw was convenient to be used as bedding for our cows. To start the straw stack, the long part of the blower was at a low horizontal angle with the nozzle directed toward the ground. As straw accumulated, the long part of the blower was raised with a hand crank. The nozzle of the blower could be adjusted up or down and back and forth as the straw stack grew in size. I watched Dad control the building of the stack using ropes running from where he stood at the apron to the nozzle of the blower. As the straw stack grew and the blower was raised, the threshing machine looked like a growing angry dragon approaching a mountain, blowing dust and making a terrible noise.

The threshing machine separated oat grains from chaff and straw. A trough delivered golden kernels of oats and was moved with a rope in an arc so the flow could be directed evenly into one of our box wagons. These small wagons had solid board sides and wooden wheels with steel rims. They were easily moved to accommodate filling and unloading. I perched on the narrow vertical sides of a box wagon to direct the trough line from where the grains spewed. No one could be in the wagon because oat grains are slippery, like quicksand, and once you are in it, you cannot get out. Some farm fatalities, including one of the Shimniok brothers on the adjacent farm, were the result of someone being suffocated by grain.

There were rules to be followed around the threshing machine, in addition to not being in the grain box. No one went near the belts when they were moving because a belt could break. I saw it happen once at Uncle Herman and Aunt Idella's farm in Minnesota. The heavy black thing took on a life of its own, snapping and coiling 20 feet in the air like a huge cobra striking out. Crack! It was like a long thick whip that could cut a man in two.

Grain was stored in our granary, the two-story southern part of the machine shed at the lower farm. I liked the clean smell of the granary because the aroma was of animal feed, not manure. The wooden floors were shiny and slippery from years of fine dust that kept them sanded smooth. Each wagon, brimming with golden oats, was hauled to the granary where the end of the box wagon was carefully opened, dropping a stream of grains into the horizontal feed line of our elevator, a heavy contraption made of surplus WWII steel. A single chain rotated the V-shaped blades, lifting grain to the big storage area on the second level of the granary. The floor of this upper level had several holes that could be plugged. On the first floor were four bins the size of stalls or small rooms. As the upper storage area filled, holes in the floor were opened to let grain flow into the small bins below, then closed when each lower bin was full, maximizing storage area for the crop. By the end of a good harvest, all the bins below were full and a reserve pile of oats was staged in the upper level of the granary.

Each lower bin was fronted with a series of flat wooden panels about a foot wide. These could be adjusted, added to or removed, as the level of grain changed. When our animals needed ground feed, Dad or Grandpa stood outside a bin to scoop oats into burlap bags, because going into full bins posed the danger of suffocation. I held the bags and sometimes rode along when Dad took them to the feed mill in Reedsburg to be ground. We also took gunny sacks of corn. Oats and dried corn on the cob were ground together to make the special ground feed our animals savored. Sometimes protein concentrate was added. Spare bags were taken along to be recycled and filled with the mix.

When we returned from the mill, the ground feed was dumped from the burlap bags into feedboxes in the barn. I scooped it on top of a mound of silage in front of each stanchion to entice our cows into the barn and keep them occupied and still while they were milked. Cows are particularly fond of ground feed.

Three or more bags of grain could be stacked on the wheeling cart in the granary and rolled to the dock for loading onto our one-and-a-half-ton truck. The cart was a great toy. When I was four years old, I stood on the foot of the cart and leaned against the back. Dad tipped the cart back and rolled me around. His quick maneuvers had me giggling in no time. The following year David joined me for these rides, then Allen; we had to squeeze together and tightly hold on to each other for the fun. The cart continued to be a great source of entertainment as I got big enough to wheel David or Allen, eventually Randy. We got daring. How fast could we go? How far back could we tip each other? Where could we wheel each other? How about on the entire driveway around the milk house? Cart entertainment waned as we all became too heavy to wheel.

 The floor scale in the granary was a big metal heavy-duty thing with a hook at the end of a horizontal balance beam at eye level. The hook had a drop rod to hang the round slotted calibrated weights. Dad had us step onto the platform, adjusted the sliding weights until the arrow floated in the space between the metal guides; he told us we were getting bigger. It made me feel grown up. Years later, after I learned about nutrition and calories and understood what a person ate was directly proportional to their weight, I revisited the scale and wondered how I was ever so naïve.

28

Corn

We rotated crops annually to maintain the nutritional content of the soil in our fields. Each crop has its unique contribution and requirements. Fields to be planted were prepared by plowing, discing and dragging. Each operation was performed using a different piece of equipment. Plowing overturned residual stubble from the crop of the previous year. We had a three bottom plow that made for many trips back and forth to till a field. Long dark smooth logs of soil were left behind the plow. The disc blades cut those packed logs into small clumps of dirt. The many tines of the wide flat drag smoothed the clumps into fine soil. The result was a smooth surface that looked like a beach. Sometimes I wrote on it with a long branch from the edge of the field.

The fertile land emitted a fresh earthy fragrance that floated across a field as it was plowed. "Stay by the buildings. Don't go in the field. Stay away from the plow." Mom shouted her warnings from the backdoor just as David was taking his first steps into the field south of our house on the upper farm.

"I wanna tell Daddy about the nightcrawlers," David hollered back.

Mom had our full attention as she marched toward us. "The plow is dangerous. Daddy can't hear you approaching over the noise of the tractor. He's watching what he's doing." When Mom talked to us this sternly, we listened.

"Daddy will remember the nightcrawlers," she assured David.

When Dad plowed the field by our house, he stopped occasionally motioning to us, and we ran out to the soil he had turned over. Dad was already behind the plow and together we picked angleworms and nightcrawlers from the pungent ground. The slippery worms and crawlers were often packed so tightly they tore apart as we pulled, and they squirmed to escape. We knew Dad would take us to the river for an hour of fishing those days. When we were 10 years old and with permission, we could go to the river ourselves while Dad and Grandpa continued to prepare the fields.

Our planter cut the soil, dropped three kernels of seed corn into evenly spaced holes about 18 inches apart and covered the seeds. Planted fields were just flat dark soil for several days. Then, especially if we had rain and warm temperatures, distinct lines of tiny green sprouts broke through the earth like a promise of something wonderful. These fields were watched carefully for places the planter missed. We walked the rows of corn with little handheld planters to fill in the gaps being sure to keep rows straight for the picker in the fall. "Knee high by the Fourth of July" was the mantra. It did not always happen, but most of the time it did.

When I was 10 years old, my tractor driving skills were deemed adequate to cultivate corn. The cultivator was mounted on a tractor and used to physically control weeds in cornfields. It had a series of shiny metal flat pointed diggers about six inches tall. They could be lowered into the soil by a lever operated by the tractor driver. The diggers were strategically placed so when one digger disrupted weeds in the soil another covered and smothered them. This was tricky work especially when corn plants were small. I drove slowly. It was easy to get too close to the corn plants and smother them along with the weeds. Given that situation, the hearty weeds usually rejuvenated, but the fragile young corn plants often died.

    I liked this new job at first and spent many long continuous hours cultivating. My critical eye watched the cornrow on the right side of the tractor. I knew if the front tractor tires were kept a specific distance from the corn plants, the rest of the tractor, including the big side tires, would not run over any of the crop and the diggers usually did not cover corn plants. Occasionally, a digger caught a large chunk of hard soil and—Bam! It landed on a little sprout of corn. I stopped the tractor on the spot when that happened and grabbed the long mop handle laying along the side of the tractor. I used it to carefully uncover the little corn plant and crunch the chunk of soil into pieces, never getting off the tractor seat.

    I learned how to turn the tractor at the end of each row of corn, minimizing the number of tiny corn plants the tractor wheels destroyed. Dad appeared in the field occasionally, "You're doing a wonderful job, Susie." I liked cultivating because I could sing and no one could hear me, or I could tell stories and makeup skits. The sun was hot by mid-morning on those summer days in late June and early July. The taller the plants grew, the faster I drove the tractor because the sturdy corn stalks could withstand most trauma inflicted by the brush of the tractor wheels or a clump of dirt pushed against them.

One day when I was about 12 years old, the oppressive heat and humidity were unbearable as I cultivated a field on the east end of the farm on the flat above the creek. Although it was early June and the plants were small, I moved the throttle up a notch, then two notches, to create my own breeze. The faster I went, the more often I had to stop to uncover small corn sprouts. The sun burned into my skin; I wanted the job to be done.

My thought of the first tiny sprout that was covered by soil, the one I did not stop to uncover, did not slip from my mind—neither did the next. "They'll be fine." I tried to convince myself. Perspiration ran down my back into my shorts. My legs and arms were red with sunburn; gnats and tiny flies buzzed through the curls around my face. Dad did not come to the field that day. He did not usually come to check on me anymore because I had been cultivating for a couple years. He had confidence in my work. When I finished cultivating the field and drove back to the barnyard, many tiny uncovered corn sprouts wrestled in my mind.

The next day on my way to collect eggs I heard, "Susie, let's go for a walk." Dad and I started through the swale, past the pig barn, across the little creek and up the hill on the makeshift road to the east fields where we stopped. I knew all along where we were going. Dad never walked with me like that.

He pulled his jackknife out of the bib of his overalls. Flick! He knelt and pushed the knife with a turn into a mound of soil where there should have been a corn plant. A tiny yellow green corn sprout appeared from under the ground. It stood at an angle like it had been injured. My lips trembled with the effort of holding back tears. I was not scared. I felt really bad.

Dad told me he would take care of the corn. I was to finish collecting eggs. I walked back to the chicken coop alone, turning around to watch Dad work his way through the field rescuing his corn crop from his daughter's foolishness. It took hours. Dad never talked about what I had done again, but the guilt never left me.

Rain and warm temperatures, both in moderation, were needed for a successful corn crop. Weather, specifically rainfall, was the main topic of conversation among area farmers. Different soils require different amounts of moisture. Corn plants show what they need. When corn leaves turn a grayish green and curl, they are clearly indicating a need for water. Cool wet weather after planting stunts plant growth; the corn would not be knee high by the Fourth of July.

Later in summer the top of the corn plant tassels and one, maybe two, small cobs sprout midway up the stalk. Pollen from the tassel falls onto the silk at the end of the cobs to pollinate the plant. Disruption of this process by aphids, beetles, disease, wind or hail could be disastrous. Fall is the next critical time corn is affected by weather. It should be relatively warm and dry, but not too warm and not too dry. By fall, kernels on a healthy corncob are full and well-formed and begin to dent and harden, but an early frost interrupts this final stage of growth. Additionally, an early heavy snowfall could prevent harvesting an otherwise successful crop. All of these variables had an impact on the nutritional content of the food we fed to our animals.

Silos were filled with silage at the end of August or early September before the corn completely hardened and while the stalks were green. Corn that had been damaged by hail or was leaning toward the ground from wind or standing in wet areas during the season was used for silage. This corn was cut in the fields and tied into bundles with the corn binder. This binder was similar to the one used for oats because it tied cut stalks into bundles. It was different because it cut only one row of the sturdy corn plants at a time. Also, bundles of corn are much bigger, heavier and not as fragile as those of oats.

Bundles of silage corn were dropped in the field, loaded onto wagons by hand and hauled to the silo where they were parked by the filler. Our first silo filler was small, as silo fillers go. There was a long narrow bed where a rotating chain apron moved a bundle of corn toward the grinder. The bed looked sinister to me because it was just the size of a grown person. I worried Dad or Grandpa would fall off the wagon into the narrow bed and shuddered with thoughts of them being fed into the grinder.

There was a belt driven wheel that made the whole thing work. The wide belt, wrapped around that wheel and around the circular belt drive on one of our tractors, was as dangerous as the grinder. My brothers and I learned early-on to stay away from belts. They could pick a grown man off his feet and toss him into the air or pull him into machinery.

After corn went through the grinder, the silage was blown up a metal tube that had been assembled along the vertical exterior of the silo. The top of this tube formed a curved arch that guided the silage into the top of the tall round structures. The top of the silo looked like a gaping mouth that was hungry until the entire thing was filled to the brim. After adding a silo to the lower farm and building the big silo on the upper farm, Dad bought a larger-capacity

Blizzard silo filler at an auction. We called it the Blizzard because we thought that was a funny name for a silo filler.

The better corn was left to ripen and harden in the field until October. Again, the binder cut and bundled the corn row by row. Men picked the bundles off the ground and assembled them into teepee-shaped corn shocks. This allowed corn to dry in the field so it would not mold as it was stored during winter. A bale of binder twine was hauled along and used to tie shocks once they were upright. It was easier when two people did the assembling because a shock was not stable until it was tied. Each held many bundles and one person could not reach around its circumference. After the twine was wrapped around a couple times, a mighty heft by the men secured it tightly and stabilized the shock upright while the corn dried. I was occasionally in the fields for shocking, although I was usually at school.

Dad told a story about one Halloween when he and his friends in Caledonia, Minnesota, first had a car. That evening after chores and well after dark, they drove to a farmer's field close to town and wrapped a chain around the bottom of a corn shock. They hooked the other end of the chain to the car. With the car lights off, they slowly and carefully drove the huge thing to the main intersection in the village where they unhooked and collected the chain. Then they quietly and slowly drove home, leaving the corn shock in·the middle of town. The village fathers were scratching their heads in the morning, thinking the shock, over ten feet tall, had been assembled on site. The corn shock was not easily identified because many such shocks stood in fields throughout Houston County. Dad claimed he and his friends were not caught that year.

The following Halloween they went back to the same farm with the same car and the chain. They wrapped the chain around the farmer's outhouse. With the car lights off, they slowly and carefully dragged the structure into the village to the same intersection. Again, they slowly drove home. The village fathers did not find this humorous at all. The outhouse was identified. Dad said when he and the boys offered to help haul the outhouse back to its proper home, he figured, "the jig was up." He chuckled all the way through that story every time he told it.

Our shocks stood a number of weeks, depending on the weather and how wet the year had been. We had to get all of the corn harvested before snow prevented us from getting it out of the fields. Binder twine holding the tall structures in place was cut and collected as the shocks were disassembled. Twine could wedge in gears and break machinery or get stuck in a cow's digestive track if ingested. When I was in the field, I was responsible for holding on to twine as shocks were taken down. It was usually windy and cold, and when twine blew away from someone, I chased after it collecting the long strings under the thumb of my mittened hand. The many strands of twine were wrapped like a heavy scarf around the back of my neck as I hauled them from the field at the end of the day.

We ran corn stalks through a shredder that looked like a small threshing machine, and like the threshing machine, belts had to be correctly placed on it. One of our tractors provided the operating drive to make it work. Twine on individual bundles was cut and stashed on a hook before the corn stalks were laid on a rotating apron that fed them into the shredder where ears of corn were stripped off the stalks and husks removed. Deep yellow cobs of corn thumped along a trough hanging off the side of the shredder and into one of the small high-sided wooden wagons, the same wagons we used for oats.

    I did not like perching on the high narrow side boards of those wagons because they hurt my backside in short order. The first time Grandpa assigned me to direct corncobs, I stood on the floor of the wagon and reached up to grab the rope directing the trough. I reassessed this tactic when the first ear of corn caught me on the side of my head. Whack! I grabbed my ear and saw the next cob flying at me, but ducked out of its path just in time. While rubbing my temple and collecting myself, I dropped the rope and a pile of cobs was stacking high on the far end of the wagon.

    Grandpa turned and hollered. "Susie, move the trough." Since Grandpa quit feeding stalks there were no cobs. I took this opportunity to dart across the wagon, grab the rope and pull the trough in my direction. Momentarily, the cobs were thumping down the trough again, but not before I hoisted myself to the high sides of the wagon and perched so I could direct the trough with the rope. I was now above the action and stayed there until the wagon was half full, and I could easily step onto the corn. The cobs now tumbled out waist high, and I could position myself around the trough and maneuver it so the cobs never hit me.

    All of the corn plant except the cob was fodder and was forced out the blower to become a huge stack. Fodder could be used for bedding or feed. When hay was in short supply due to drought, the fodder was blown directly into the barn loft on the upper farm to keep it dry and in good condition for feeding the youngstock. Wagons full of corn on the cob were unloaded into our cribs. Corncribs were long, tall narrow buildings with slatted wooden sides to let the wind blow through, allowing corn to continue to dry.

The elevator used for lifting grain into the granary was also used to move corn into the cribs. The elevator made an awful noise. Metal moving across metal created a terrible screeching sound; my ears rang for 15 minutes after it stopped. Once in a while, Dad put a lot of oil on it while unloading corn by our house on the upper farm. I think he did that so the neighbors would not complain, not so it would be quieter for us.

We quit using the shredder when dad bought the corn picker that mounted unto the model M Farmall tractor. It was a two-row corn picker, its top speed something close to plodding. Cobs of ripe corn dropped one at a time into the wagon being towed. Both the corn picker and the shredder were prone to getting plugged. This consumed valuable time because the power shafts and belts had to be disengaged before a plug could be removed. We knew more than one farmer who lost fingers, a hand or an arm because they were in a hurry and did not disengage the power to farm machinery before they tried to remove a plug.

The corn picker replaced the corn binder and shredder just as the baler replaced the hay loader. Later the combine replaced the grain binder and threshing machine. These changes happened during my last summers on the farm or later.

Grandpa Louie came kicking and screaming into the twentieth century. He did not like the baler because too many clover seeds and too much chaff were lost in the fields. He did not like the combine because any straw baled in the fields was only stalk and not nutritious or absorbent without the chaff. He did not like the corn picker because none of the fodder, now only stalks, was usable. In addition, all of the new equipment left more crop in the field than, "doing it the right way." He harped on it daily.

There was an old corn sheller in the tool area on the second floor of the pig barn. It was a machine where one would stand in the front and shove corncobs into it while turning the crank, but it was just a novelty to us kids. David and Allen used it as a toy by turning the hand crank, pretending they were actually shelling corn. The handle turned easily, but became a real effort for the boys when they tried to shell an ear of corn. Their effort increased when doing more than one cob at a time. The boys managed to shell a cob or two just to say they did it. The kernels fell out of the bottom into a pail. The cobs worked their way up and out of an opening toward the middle of the machine. I was satisfied with just cranking the thing. Dad said he used the sheller for preparing seed corn, but that was before I could remember.

There was a pouch of strychnine poison hanging on a hook high on the wall in the machine shed at the lower farm. Things that were hanging out of reach and labeled "poison" drew my attention every time I walked by. The strychnine was added to seed corn to deter birds from eating seeds out of newly planted fields. Allen saw it on some of the seeds one time and told me the stuff was purplish in color. Later, and with permission, Allen said he and David "took the .22 rifle hanging in the shed area of the pig barn and took care of a lot of birds eating seed corn out of our fields."

Threshing oats at the upper farm.

A two-row corn picker replaced the binder on the Schroeder farm. Harold levels the corn in the box wagon that was pulled behind the picker to catch the cobs.

29

Hired Men and Uncle Louie

Dad hired men to help with the harvest. When the Shimnioks, from the farm across the railroad tracks, experienced a mechanical breakdown and their hired men could not work until the machines were repaired, they let us use their workers. Their men did not seem to mind. I think that is because no one ever left our farm hungry. Men that had helped Dad on the Schroeder family farm in Caledonia, Minnesota, occasionally drove the hundred miles to lend a hand. My cousin Tom came, too.

Hired men sweat a lot. Rivers of perspiration ran from under their straw hats and dripped from their hair onto their shoulders when they came from the fields. Shirts were soaked through to the backs of their overalls. They smelled of hard work and dirty clothes as they rested on the grassy slope of the backyard. Some sat while others lay flat in the shade of the big elm trees. Cloth handkerchiefs, already wet with perspiration, were pulled from pockets to mop faces and wipe necks.

Our old oak table on the porch off the kitchen was stretched long when we had hired men to feed. "Come on in. There's a cool breeze through the porch. Food is on the table. There's lemonade, too. You can rest after you eat."

Mom did not want the men to fall asleep before they ate; however, they never required much encouragement when it came to food. Baked chicken, ham and roast beef raised and butchered on our farm, sweet corn, carrots, beets, green beans and other vegetables from our gardens, Jell-O salads with fruit or grated carrots, and bars, cakes and pies were served with plenty to go around.

Uncle Louie was my favorite hired man. He was not my uncle, but all of my real uncles lived in Minnesota, so Mom and Dad said it was okay to call him Uncle. Louie Mielke was a bachelor and lived where he could. At one time he lived in a little one room split log shanty in a swale off of County Road W between Farview and Pikes Peak Roads, southeast of the village. He did not drive, so Mom picked him up and took him home. I rode along and occasionally saw inside his home because I was expected to help carry food that Mom packed up for Uncle Louie. I liked the strangeness of Louie's shanty, but I would not want to live there. There was no electricity or indoor plumbing.

Uncle Louie was a small man, barely coming to Mom's shoulder. He had a beard and long gray hair that Mom cut. He wore striped overalls that Mom patched. He was the person Dad hired first because he was available.

Uncle Louie stuttered and smelled of garlic. Someone told him garlic was good for your health so he wore a little leather pouch of it around his neck. When he moved to town, he walked to our house with the staples he received from the welfare folks, and with the usual westerly breeze to his back, we could smell him coming a block away.

"H-Hi g-g-irl-l-ly." He always called me girly. "Is P-P-ear-rly h-home?" We let him in with his flour, sugar, lard and various treasures.

"P-P-ear-rly, l-l-ook at the b-b-beautif-ful s-stuff I g-g-got."

Mom praised what he brought, and later added what was needed to turn it into tasty warm meals. Sometimes she baked a small pie filled with leftover slices of meat, gravy and vegetables. She loaded it in the car with warm bread, some bars or cookies, maybe some rice pudding along with one of us kids to help deliver it to Louie's small shed house off Lieder Street, close to the canning factory. I am quite sure he did not realize Mom added the extras. He assumed she could magically transform his meager fare into these wonderful treats.

One hot, humid day between harvests, Dad had Uncle Louie help him on a project at the Forty, where we pastured our youngstock during summer. These 40 acres were up in the bluffs about three and a half miles south of the farm. They were digging a hole for a small pond. As Dad tired from the work and heat, he looked over at the old man.

"Hey there, Louie. You better sit down and rest. I don't want you to have a heart attack and die on me up here."

Uncle Louie paused and looked around. "Th-there c-c-couldn't b-be a b-better sp-p-ot." He kept digging.

A good part of Uncle Louie's welfare check was spent at Dale's Bar uptown. After his ration of drinks, he pushed a hunk of Peachy chewing tobacco in the side of his mouth and headed for the door. Occasionally, some of the older boys played a game where they took bets on how many times they could lure Louie back into the bar by buying him another drink.

"Hey Louie. Why don't we get you another one?"

When this happened, the old man dug the Peachy out of his mouth and chucked it into a pocket in his overalls until he finished his free drink.

The boys always waited until Louie pulled the slimy chew from his overalls and poked it back into his mouth before they made the next offer. This could be repeated several times until either the boys ran out of money or Louie gave up. There were no winners or losers to this game. Each side got what they wanted.

When spring thaw and rains flooded our ponds by the river, Uncle Louie was watching. He told Dad, "Th-there's f-fish in the p-p-ponds. Th-they b-be g-get'n st-st-stranded when the w-w-water g-goes d-down. I c-could c-c-catch some. Sm-m-moke'm. They g-g-onna d-d-die any w-way."

He was savvy, because he started using his rifle instead of a fish pole. He did not need to hit a fish. The concussion of water brought them to the surface. Louie and Dad smoked suckers and carp. We ate some big northern pike, too.

Uncle Louie had a real nephew, an adult that visited. When he was getting older, Louie told us his nephew asked him if he had "made arrangements." Uncle Louie shot him a look. "Wh-what'ch you m-m-mean?"

"You know, do you have money set aside for your funeral, a cemetery plot, a marker? You know, to bury you. Those things cost money."

Louie pulled himself up tall and told us he pointed out to his nephew. "N-n-ever s-seen a d-d-dead one on t-top y-y-yet."

At the end, Uncle Louie had been caretaker of the Rock Hill Cemetery on County Road W for so long he was given a grave for his burial, one of the last ones.

Louie Mielke died on June 24, 1969, his birthday. He was 81 years old. I was already married in 1969. It was late when I got home from work the day before the funeral. My husband worked evenings, so I went to Louie's visitation alone. I was the only visitor at the funeral home. His tiny body was lying in a small plain wooden box. I smiled when I saw him because he was cleaned up. He looked at peace. His work was done.

Top: Louie Mielke and David Schroeder stand in front of the dock of the granary on the lower farm. David is holding his fishpole and a northern pike he caught. *Bottom*: L to R: Robert Dierson, is with Carolyn's cousin, Tom Schroeder. The boys drove over a hundred miles, from Caledonia, Minnesota, to visit and lend a hand on the farm.

Carolyn holding her little brother Randy's hand in front of the bobsled that was loaded with manure from the barn on the upper farm in the spring of 1959 following the blizzard. The family's workhorses are pulling the sled. Rex, the farm dog, is in the foreground. Rex seldom ventured from the lower farm, but the horses and the snow apparently intrigued him, and he was allowed the trip.

Animals

30

Cows

Chopped corn stored in our silos was called silage. It settled into the tall vertical structures as winter approached. Using a wide fork with multiple closely spaced tines, we loosened it from the curved walls of the silos. Silage was tossed down a chute as needed to feed our cows. The chutes were constructed down the exterior walls of the silos. These structures were attached to the barns on the upper and lower farms.

Silage froze to the walls of the silos during winter. When that happened Dad used a pickaxe as an ice chipper to loosen it to prevent accumulation. If silage froze high up on silo walls, it fell when temperatures rose. This could seriously hurt or kill anyone working beneath it. Suffocation was a real possibility.

Silage, as it ages, takes on the fragrance of a large pot of food that has turned sour. The stink can become overwhelming in spring as temperatures warm. The smell lingered in our hair and clung to our clothes. This concerned me because I did not want to smell like stinky, sour silage in a classroom on a warm spring day.

I took my turn tossing silage out of the silos. This was followed by another chore in the big barn at the lower farm. A heavy forkful of silage was lugged to the front of each cow's stanchion. A shiny metal pan was used to scoop ground feed from the small bin in front of the horse stalls; the ground feed was dumped on top of the mound of silage. Food for the cows was always prepared before they were let into the barn because it lured them through the opened door. Milking did not begin until they were in their stanchions.

In winter when the cows could not feed on pasture grasses and were stanchioned for long periods of time, loose hay that had been tossed from the mow was forked into their feed lines to be munched on between milkings. They were let outside for a drink of water and to meander the barnyard while the barn was cleaned of their waste. Their silage and ground feed were prepared again during this time.

Cows rank as some of the dumbest animals in the world; chickens are not overly bright either. This is only my opinion, but nothing has happened over the years to change my mind. Cows are eating and pooping machines. During summer, the herd grazes in the pasture until they are rounded up to the barnyard twice daily for milking. With appetites partially satisfied, they are lured into the milking parlor with ground feed. Although the herd sometimes traveled as a group, they often walked single file on paths that crisscrossed our pasture, balancing their huge bodies on skinny legs and hooves along cow paths, some well over a foot deep.

Each cow walks to a specific stanchion twice daily, year in and year out, but for some unknown reason on a random night, one cow forgets where to go. She stops and stands there with a dazed look on her face. At that moment, all of the other cows do the same thing. Not one cow can remember where to go, and spontaneously they all start to poop and pee right where they stand.

If you are extremely lucky, they figure it out. If you are not, which usually happens, the cows panic and kick. They kick each other and anyone in their way. When this happened, Dad maneuvered the cows out of the barn into the yard, and we started all over again. The cows kicked Dad on several occasions, and also my brothers and Grandpa, too. Fortunately, I was never kicked, but I remember seeing deep purple and black bruises the size of a hoof on Dad when Mom applied cold compresses. Sometimes those kicks made Dad limp for weeks. We heard of other farmers that suffered broken bones, usually on their legs, from being kicked by their cows.

Cows like consistency, and when they have been agitated they do not give milk as usual. Any disruption of milking schedules and any change in a cow's temperament may decrease the amount of milk the cow gives or alter the consistency of their milk. This, in turn, affects family income.

Cleaning gutters was one of my regular jobs at the lower farm. Gutters—shallow trenches in the cement floor of the barn—caught manure. They ran behind the cows as they stood in their stanchions. Loose straw was used to line the gutters to prevent cow manure from splattering, this was especially important during milking operations.

A fork was used to clean up solid waste followed by a shovel for liquid waste. Manure was tossed into the manure bucket that maneuvered on a track above the center cement walk between the milk lines. When the bucket was full, it was pushed on the track out of the south door into the barnyard where the manure spreader stood. There, the trigger on the bucket was unlatched and the load of manure spilled into the spreader. A tractor pulled the spreader to a field where a lever activated a chain apron to incrementally move manure to the rotating tines at the back of the spreader. From there manure was thrown backwards by the two upper beaters and sideways by the spiral widespread as the tractor traversed the field. The result was an evenly fertilized field.

Heavy snow and extremely cold weather complicated everything. Fresh manure is warm, and if possible, was hauled to the field before it froze. However, our tractors could not maneuver the spreader to the fields in deep snow. Also, the chain apron of the spreader could freeze, and the chain could break. The worst scenario was when manure froze in the spreader. During the coldest part of winter, manure was dropped in a pile in the back of the barnyard to be hand-loaded and spread in the spring. During the spring, after the Blizzard of 1959, Dad manually loaded manure from the barnyards onto the big wooden bobsled and used our horses to pull it to the fields where he manually unloaded the manure.

Our youngstock were housed in the small barn at the upper farm during the winter. In summer they were transported to the Forty, 40 acres of grass and woodland in the bluffs south of the village. During summer, the herd had to be checked and have their water refreshed frequently. We carried water to the young cows in 10-gallon pails. They were enticed to the corral with a serving of ground feed. Dad counted the youngstock as they arrived at the corral. They were usually all there, but sometimes one or more were missing.

A single cow was known to jump a low spot in the fence. Some got tangled in downed wire; hunters or other trespassers occasionally crossed the fence to our property. The cows could crowd if spooked and push a fence down allowing the whole herd to wander freely. Cattle rustlers were rare in our area, and our landlocked property presented obstacles for them. However, cows could be coerced with ground feed and water to follow anyone, anywhere, anytime. Predators occasionally killed youngstock, picking on the most vulnerable animals first. There were also diseases that could affect a single cow or the whole herd. Each of these situations required an immediate remedy.

Our cows required constant attention and were a lot of work. However, their redeeming features were nutritious milk, sweet cream, butter and cheese.

 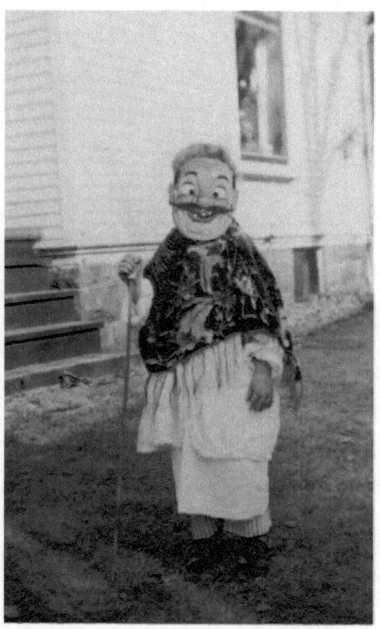

Reedsburg, Wisconsin, started daytime trick or treat hours for Halloween in the mid-1950s. Carolyn was invited to visit her great aunts, Martha (Beckman) Janzen and Emma Beckman, to participate in the event. Carolyn dressed in a Halloween costume she fashioned from her great aunt's old clothes. Her first store bought mask was a gift from Martha.

31

The Bull

Dairy operations were our primary source of income. We milked about thirty head of Holstein cows in the big barn on the lower farm. We had a bull early on, but later our cows were artificially inseminated. The bull was usually at the lower farm. However, one fall he had been in the field south of our home on the upper place grazing on cornstalks, the remains of a recently harvested field. He had a ring in his nose, attached to a metal chain with sturdy links that was attached to a large heavy cement ball. He was docile, but my brothers and I were told, "Stay away!"

That same fall, when our bull was tethered in the upper field, we experienced an exceptionally memorable Halloween. The previous year I had been invited to visit my great aunts, Martha and Emma, who lived in Reedsburg, the town northwest of us. Reedsburg started daytime trick-or-treat hours in the mid-1950s. Martha and Emma let me shuffle through their box of old clothes to make a costume. I selected a colorful shawl to wear over a shirt that was way too big. A tall cane completed the outfit.

I was excited when Martha handed my first store bought mask to me. It was a man's face; he looked like a happy baker with a mustache and a few missing teeth. I ran to the big round mirror on her dressing table and pulled the mask over my head to cover my face. It looked great in the mirror—what I could see of it. Elastic string held the thick cardboard close against my nose and lashes. The eyeholes were not made for my eyes so I could peek out of only one eyehole at a time. I did not want to hurt Martha's feelings, so I did not whine. After all, she bought the mask for me.

My picture was taken wearing the costume before Martha suggested I take the mask off so I could see—what a relief! She painted my lips and cheeks with lipstick. I rode home with Mom when the event finished and got to trick-or-treat again in North Freedom.

The discarded mask was all but forgotten the following Halloween. I was 10 years old; my brothers were nine and eight. We conjured costumes from our bag of old clothes and adopted Martha's plan of coloring our lips and cheeks with lipstick. Mom gave us a tube of zinc oxide to smear white on our faces. David found a small chunk of coal in the bin and we outlined our eyes with black. In past years our masks were brown paper bags. Holes were cut in the bags for our eyes and mouth, loppy ears were formed of construction paper, and dry corn silk was pasted on for eyebrows, maybe a mustache. This year we did not fiddle with masks. We painted our faces, slammed on hats and proceeded to trick or treat.

Each year Mom allowed us to go a bit further from home as long as we were together. Upon our return we each were given a cake pan for our candy. We were allowed to eat three pieces at a time so I sorted through my loot and placed the biggest candy bars on one side with my personal favorites in the upper left corner. The smaller, less desirable pieces were on the right. My special arranging helped stretch my favorite candy over time; I picked one favorite and two others assuring a favorite was available for weeks.

As I sorted through my mound of treats that evening, Elsie Worth from next door came knocking; there was a call for us. We did not have a telephone. Mom trucked off to Elsie and Dan's to take the call. She was laughing when she returned, as she explained folks uptown had reported seeing someone dressed up like a bull. The costume was very real looking. They saw it nosing around the grocery stores and meat locker. We were to make sure our bull was okay.

"We would have heard if someone hurt our bull. He's just beyond the back yard." Mom was confident. "On the other hand, it is Halloween." She glanced at Dad who chuckled at the story as he walked toward the back door. He was gone only a short time before the backdoor flung wide open, and Dad tore into the house.

"The bull is gone. The cement ball is there. The bull is gone!" Dad was puzzled. Where was our bull?

Momentarily befuddled, Dad and Mom looked at each other not knowing whether to laugh or cry. Did someone take him? We had heard no commotion. Or—heaven forbid! Could our bull be walking around uptown—on Halloween?

"This is a serious situation," Dad muttered as he pulled on his jacket and ran to the barn.

He grabbed two galvanized pails and scooped a big helping of ground feed into the smallest pail. The bigger pail he half filled with water. With the pails in the back of the truck and watching in every direction for our bull, Dad slowly headed uptown.

He felt he needed Grandpa's help to find the large animal and bring him home. He stopped at Franklin Street, got out and shown the flashlight toward Grandma and Grandpa's terrace. No bull. He crawled up the terrace and jogged kitty corner across the empty lot to their backdoor. There were no lights on in the house that he could see. He pounded on the door to no avail. Dad reconsidered searching for the bull on his own, but he did not think that was a good idea. He shuffled in the dark to the bedroom window and pounded some more.

Grandpa was not happy about having his sleep interrupted in such an abrupt manner. "Who's out there? What the hell you want? What's going on?" he growled through the narrowly opened lower sash of the double hung panes. He could not initially determine who was pounding outside in the dark.

Grandpa roused quickly when Dad told him about the bull. He even said it was a good thing Dad thought to bring ground feed and water. The big guy could be enticed with the familiar aromas. They hurried to the truck, each grabbed a pail and started walking uptown.

The bull actually found the men once he smelled ground feed. Dad handed the pail he carried to Grandpa, who turned around and started walking east on Walnut Street toward the farm. The bull caught up quickly with a rattled snort, but Grandpa did not hurry even though the bull occasionally nudged the pail of ground feed. Grandpa knew fast actions might agitate the big guy who had already had quite an adventure. Dad cautiously walked alongside the pair for a while before he bent to the ground and grabbed the end of the broken chain. In this most uneventful style, the men walked the huge animal home.

The trio did not stop at the upper farm but walked straight to the lower place in the moonlight where our bull was secured in his stall. That was the end of our bull. He would go on to service another herd of cows at a different farm.

32

Pigs

We raised pigs for sale and butchering. Our pigs were housed in a three-story building that Grandpa built in the mid to late 1930s, right at the beginning of the Great Depression. The pigs were on the lower level. The ceiling of the lower level was made of wooden boards. It served as the floor of the second level. The smell of the pigs floated up and through the cracks between the boards and wafted throughout the building.

Pig-sized flap doors allowed the pigs to enter and exit the building at their leisure. Outside in their pen was a slop trough that Dad and Grandpa maintained. They stirred a special mixture of ground feed and water to make slop.

A wood-fired cooker kept the pigs warm in cold weather. They do not produce body heat like cows. The cooker also heated water so the pigs could have warm slop in winter. It was made of a three-foot-wide piece of sheet metal welded in a ring for a base. A big cast iron pot that looked like a huge kettle rested on its rim.

Cob corn from our cribs was lugged in a galvanized metal basket along the makeshift road that went toward the creek to a short cement wall that secured our pigs. The cobs were dumped over the wall into the deep pen on the other side.

The pigs snuffled and squealed eager to get to their food; I never heard pigs make an oink sound.

The creek ran along the east side of the pig barn toward the pasture and on to the river. Older pigs lumbered their huge bodies on tiny hooves across the pen toward the creek to lie in the mud—snuffling all the way. Mud and cold creek water cooled them on hot summer days.

When baby piglets arrived, Dad carefully arranged them to nurse so their mother would not lie on them and crush them. As the tiny piglets grew, they were constantly active and noisy, especially at feeding time. They ran and squealed to be first to nurse and raced to the trough to gorge on slop. Pigs are always hungry.

Unlike our cows that gave milk and chickens that laid eggs, we raised pigs only as food—for our family and for sale. Their redeeming features were smoked ham, bacon, pork chops, steaks, and sausage.

33

Chickens

We raised chickens for eating and for their eggs. Our baby chicks were ordered through the mail. The Chicago & Northwestern train transported them to North Freedom, where they arrived in special shipping boxes with holes for air. Their peep, peep, peep could be heard throughout the post office. After Grandma and Grandpa moved from the lower farmhouse to their home on Franklin Street, one room of their old house was used for our baby chicks.

We entered the vacant old house on the lower farm through the now decrepit, dark moss-covered boards of the summer kitchen to care for the chicks. The steps to the kitchen were still intact, and the kitchen itself looked like it did when Grandma and Grandpa lived there. A few glasses still sat in the cupboard with glass doors in the pantry. The small room on the south side of the kitchen was the baby chick room and was divided in half with chicken wire fencing. A heat lamp was hung from the ceiling on one side for warmth. The chicks had to be watched carefully as they were placed on the side with the heat lamp. It was not unusual to lose a couple of them for any number of reasons. They were already stressed from transport. They occasionally clustered for warmth and smothered one another. The worst case scenario was for the entire flock to develop a disease, but that rarely happened.

The chicks grew quickly, and their downy yellow bodies started to develop stiff white feathers. Those that developed feathers first were separated to the opposite side of the wire fencing to prevent them from injuring the smaller birds. Chickens are social and instinctively develop a hierarchy within the flock. The bigger and stronger birds become aggressive toward those smaller and weaker. We were concerned some of our smaller chicks would not survive this natural pecking order so we separated them from birds that were growing feathers.

The chicken coop was a long narrow building between the house and the pig barn. The west wall and later a short part of the north was divided into small nesting compartments filled with straw that we changed out regularly. They reminded me later of a shoe store, or rather a shoe store reminded me of the chicken coop because of the way the compartments were structured. The rest of the north wall to the east was a roosting area made of a series of narrow boards fashioned like an upright collapsible clothes rack. It dripped with and smelled of chicken manure. The south side was windows.

Chickens laid their eggs in the nesting compartments. Eggs were collected daily in a small galvanized pail. I had no problem picking up eggs if there were no chickens sitting on the nests, but wore a lightweight work glove for two reasons. First, eggs sometimes had manure on them, and I did not want to touch it. Second, hens found sitting on eggs sometimes use vicious pecking to defend their stash.

Chickens typically lay one egg per day, and even though many nests were available, it was not unusual for several chickens to use the same nest. There could be 10 or more eggs in one nesting compartment. Invariably a motherly hen decided to sit on the eggs in one of these nests requiring me to slowly reach under her warm body and carefully retrieve each egg individually lest I break one. As my hand slid under her, this hen cocked her head so one eye locked on me. It was at this point the hen often delivered a spontaneous peck. Hens had an uncanny knack of striking my arm just above the protection of the glove leaving a bloody dent in my skin. Occasionally, a setting hen flew straight at me as I reached under her. The first time that happened I almost dropped an entire pail of eggs.

   The eggs were taken to our home at the upper farm for cleaning, sorting and packing into wooden crates. All of these tasks were done by hand. I helped with this job starting at age eight. Each egg was checked. Cracked, very small and very large eggs were used for baking, cooking and eating. Clean eggs were packed for sale into wooden crates with collapsible cardboard dividers. Dirty eggs were wiped clean with a wet cloth, dried and crated. Very dirty eggs were placed in a small pail of water to soak until all other eggs had been crated. Extremely dirty eggs, those with chunks of crusted manure stuck to them, were soaked in a vinegar and water solution and were the last to be cleaned. The concentration of vinegar and the length of time eggs were immersed in the solution were critical because vinegar is an acid which chemically softens eggshells. Mom usually used these eggs rather than selling them because stains of manure were often still visible.

   We worked with bare hands, no rubber gloves. Occasionally Mom took our eggs to Brook's egg business on Maple Street uptown. However, she usually sold the eggs to C. W. Hawes Egg Company on Water Street in

North Freedom

Baraboo because they paid more money. These companies inspected inside each egg by showing a light behind them in a dark room. This is called candling because originally candles provided the light. Bloody whites, blood spots and opaqueness, indicating bacteria, could be seen inside the eggs because the light shown through the shells.

After selling the eggs to Hawes, Mom stopped at Gardener's Bakery in Baraboo where she bought a bag or two of day-old baked goods: bread, rolls, and coffeecakes. Deliverymen regularly replaced unsold product off grocery store shelves with fresh baked goods. Gardener's packaged their old product in big two-ply paper bags and retailed it at bargain prices. These bags were the size of gunny sacks. We ate old bread. It was perfectly fine. Mom used dried out baked goods for stuffing or delicious bread pudding which she served with a sauce created from our own dairy fresh cream, sugar, and vanilla from the Watkins man.

Our Watkins man stopped by our home in his personal vehicle. It held hundreds of treasures homemakers could not do without, especially spices; the Watkins company was well known for their spices. After Mom and folks in the village made their purchases, the man continued his route throughout the countryside. Many people in remote rural areas depended on their Watkins man because they had little opportunity to shop in town.

My brothers and I shuffled through these bags of old bread as soon as Mom returned home, hoping to find a cream filled coffee cake. I could almost eat a whole cake myself.

"I get the first one," David said as he pawed through the baked goods. David was more aggressive than Allen and me, but we were stealthier in the way we defended ourselves against him.

"Don't squish the bread." Mom stepped in to supervise. "If there's a coffee cake in either bag, you'll all share." There was seldom more than one coffee cake in a bag, and often there was none.

We were assigned jobs while Mom was selling eggs in Baraboo. She wrote these assignments on the backs of envelopes saved from opened mail for just such a purpose. Allen and I had household duties. David was often assigned outside work with Dad, who stayed on the farm while Mom was gone. This meant David was usually not around when Mom returned with the bags of baked goods.

"It's a good thing David is outside so he doesn't squish the bread," my self-righteous tone of voice exuded authority. Mom gave me the eagle eye of disapproval, but did not disagree. Allen smiled.

We always shared the coffee cakes with David, but Allen and I were not so sure he would have returned that favor.

34

Good Eating

We butchered six to ten chickens at a time, sometimes more. Grandpa chopped off their heads with a short-handled ax. When they were done flopping about, the bodies were dipped in a bucket of scalding water to loosen the stiff white feathers. Mom pulled off the steaming hot feathers in big handfuls. I pulled pinfeathers, those tiny little growths which were not mature enough to be released with the long feathers. Mom singed the plucked bodies over the flame of the gas stove in the kitchen to burn off hair and organic material. We used a sturdy red-handled pair of scissors to cut the chickens into pieces for cleaning and cooking.

    I loosened the gooey insides by running my thumb along the ribcage of a carcass. The heart, liver, and gizzard, called giblets, were easily separated from the intestines. The edible muscle part of the gizzard had to be separated from the crunchy part. The gizzard is actually a separate muscular stomach that uses previously swallowed stones or hard material to further digest food because chickens do not have teeth. Feeders containing chicken grit sat by the coop to provide this dietary requirement to our flock. Oyster shells were supplemented to harden eggshells and strengthen bones. Giblets were a delicacy when simmered in water, butter, and seasoning.

Mom cooked chicken by browning and roasting it on top of the gas stove, not in the oven. Her techniques turned the meanest old birds into tasty dinners; many became soup. I never felt bad for the chickens I ate because I remembered the nasty pecks on my arm delivered by the hens guarding their nests.

We butchered one cow and two pigs each fall. Everyone was involved. Most of the work was performed in the new double garage at the upper farm. Large chunks of meat were cleaned, cut with sturdy handsaws, wrapped in freezer paper and labeled for storage in one of our locker boxes at Vater's Locker Plant uptown. Grandma and Grandpa rented their own locker box for their share of the meat. Later in the year, Mom or Dad stopped by the locker to pick up whatever cut of meat was needed for meals. When I was older, I, too, picked up meat from our locker drawers.

Gay and Erna Vater first had a tiny cubby store off Maple Street in the back of the big building on the southeast corner of Walnut Street uptown. At that location, they, as the proprietors, needed to go to our box and collect our meat. When the post office moved from the front of that large building to a new structure across the street, Vater's expanded their business into that vacant space. In this larger area, we collected our own meat, but we first needed to ask Gay or Erna for the keys to our boxes. They kept close control of them so no one could claim "missing meat" due to a "lost or stolen key."

While Mom took the wrapped pieces of fine cuts of meat to the locker, Grandpa and Dad worked with the bony chunks and small pieces of meat that had been trimmed while sawing. They cooked this meat, bones and all, in big pots sitting on the wood stove on the south wall of the garage. The cow's neck and head were boiled in a large copper kettle; it was the only pot big enough to hold the massive pieces. Meat easily fell off the bones after cooking.

Some of these cooked trimmings were added to Mom's already canned vegetable soup, then canned again as vegetable beef soup. Residual water from boiling bones to release meat was saved as starter stock or broth. The enticing aroma of butchering wafted to the house and throughout the yard for several days.

Different cuts of meat were reserved for sausage. The innards of animals were removed and stripped of waste to be used as sausage casings. Long sections of intestines were taken to Vater's Locker Plant where they were cut, properly cleaned and otherwise prepared. Gay and Erna sold casings they received from other farmers who did not use them.

I was about 10 years old when I finally understood where sausage casings came from. This caused me to hesitate before I took the next bite of sausage. However, it tasted so good my squeamish thoughts were quickly squelched. Eventually we bought casings that were commercially produced.

Hunks of sausage meat were fed into a heavy grinder mounted on the large wooden butchering table. Dad's or Grandpa's strong arms turned the crank because the task required great effort. To minimize their work, they eventually attached a pulley to the grinder and mounted a three-quarter-horse motor to the table. In some cases, like Mettwurst, the sausage was a combination of beef and pork. After combining the meats and adding spices, a batch of this sausage was mixed by hand.

Once the ground raw meat was prepared, Dad or Grandpa used a utensil called a casing stuffer that looked very much like the grinder. A casing was pushed all the way onto the tube of the stuffer to fill the far end first. A crank forced the sausage meat into the casing that was eased off the tube as it filled with meat. It was important to keep air from getting into a casing because air in the casing caused the sausage to spoil. To remove bubbles, the person filling the casing used their fingers to vent air by pushing each bubble along the length of the sausage to the outer ends. The crank was difficult to turn because of the integrity of the meat. The required maneuvering of the casing further complicated the task. Dad and Grandpa eventually mounted a half-horse motor to operate the casing stuffer. Each casing was packed solid with meat: blood sausage, headcheese and Mettwurst, the pork and beef summer sausage. When they were full, both ends of each casing were tied and knotted with string. If bubbles were found after the casings were tied, those bubbles were pricked with a pin or sharp toothpick to vent the air.

The long sausage sticks were taken to Vater's where Gay and Erna placed them in their smokehouse. Mom stored the smoked sausages in a cool spot, either the back porch or the basement; our refrigerator was too small to hold all that sausage. It was a staple for sandwiches for the five or six of us and Grandma and Grandpa through the winter and early spring. My great aunts: Martha, Emma and Alma were each given a stick. The sausage was always all gone before the weather turned warm.

Kopfwurst was a special kind of preserved meat not packed in casings. Kopfwurst means "head sausage," and was made by boiling the head and neck of the cow in our oblong copper cooker to loosen the meat from the bone. This meat was then scraped away and added to other scraps of meat removed from bones and mixed in a huge kettle. Mom and Grandma spooned and patted the brownish-gray mixture tightly into cake pans, let it cool, cut it into wedges, wrapped it in wax paper and took it to our locker box.

Kopfwurst was served as a hot mound of meat and was my favorite because of the unique allspice flavor. Each sausage required different spices. I did not see Dad or Grandpa using printed recipes, but the flavors of each sausage were consistent from year to year. Dad and Grandpa each had their own combination of spices and meat mixtures. They did not share their secrets.

Liverwurst was made in the same way as kopfwurst. The only difference was the use of pork liver instead of meat from the cow's head and neck. Otherwise, it had the same spices and was prepared and packaged in the same way. Homemade liverwurst tasted nothing like store bought Braunschweiger or ring liver sausage. It was much sweeter and spicier. We spread it on bread for a snack and later had liverwurst and strawberry jelly sandwiches. They were a treat that cannot be duplicated.

Tongue, beef liver and brains were not preserved. Rather they were served as tasty quick meals during the days of butchering. Tongues were boiled, seasoned and sliced for snacks and sandwiches. Beef liver was sliced, dipped in flour, fast fried in butter and onions and served for lunch, dinner or sometimes breakfast after morning chores. Brains, Dad's favorite, looked like gray scrambled eggs. Ample tongue and liver lasted several days. Brains lasted only one meal. Nothing was wasted.

Allen and David Schroeder, with Skippy, the little black lamb.

35

Skippy and the Geese

John and Elsie Shimniok owned the adjacent farm across the tracks and to the north. One day John and Elsie's son, Ernie, brought a little black lamb to our house. It had been born on his farm. Ernie said his three kids were squabbling over wanting to care for it so Ernie said it was ours. The lamb was small and delicate and required special attention. It stayed on the upper farm and had to be fed with a baby bottle. My brothers and I knew from day one the little lamb was for all three of us to share. My brothers and I called him Skippy. He was the only animal we were ever allowed to name. We nursed the little lamb along, and he grew. When he became too big to be a pet, Dad gave Skippy back to Ernie.

As children, we were highly discouraged from naming our animals or treating them as pets. We were taught to respect our farm animals as an important part of what made the farm function. Our parents did not discuss details of farm finances with my brothers and me. However, it was generally known to us that the farm brought in $10,000 annually and $9,000 of that had to be reinvested in the farm. This left $1,000 each year for us to live on. As children, we understood our family depended on our animals for income, and we treated them accordingly.

North Freedom

For several years Mom and Dad kept two white geese at the first corner of our half mile road, one for Thanksgiving dinner and one for Christmas. The geese were part of Ruth Licht's flock. Ruth was one of the Shimniok girls, Ernie's sister.

My brothers and I took turns bringing food and water to these big birds. The heavy old wooden gate on the corner had to be hauled open and secured in place each time we tended the geese. They were mean; with lowered heads and outstretched necks, they ran at me honking. It was not possible to outmaneuver them. I thought about setting them free when their strong clipped wings beat my legs and arms—I never did. But I never felt bad enjoying those holiday dinners.

36

Rex

We had one farm dog at a time. They were all named Rex. Dad and Grandpa agreed on that because they felt it was important each new farm dog knew his name right off as he was trained to work with our cows. The men knew they would continue to call a new dog Rex even if he had a different name. The process of changing their habit would frustrate them and confuse a new dog. My brothers and I were not involved in naming our dogs. Rex's job was to round up cows from the pasture and bring them to the barn for milking. Each Rex knew our herd.

The Baraboo River was the long curved southern boundary of our lowland pasture; much of our pasture was not visible from the lower farm. With his hands cupped around his mouth Dad called, "Com'bas! Com'bas!" from the barnyard at milking time. This alerted not only our cows but Rex too, and the dog tore to the pasture to bring the herd home.

Sometimes one or more cows would not arrive with the others. Rex usually knew where the strays were stranded or where they decided to hang out and led Dad to them. Dad's command "Go get'm Rex" signaled the dog to head out in the direction of the missing cows.

Following heavy downpours or long stretches of rain, one or more of our animals could get stuck in mud in the lowland pasture. Dad had to rescue them. When fresh green grass was bountiful, some cows preferred continuing to munch in the pasture, reluctant to walk to the barn for milking. If they were not stuck, they usually came to the barn after some serious coaxing by Rex that involved a lot of circling and barking, maybe a nip at a tail. Dad tagged after the dog to assist with persistently errant animals. When pasture grass was green and bellies were full, the aroma of a small scoop of ground feed provided enough encouragement for the strays to return to the barn.

The Rexes were not allowed in the house. They usually stayed at the lower farm. I mostly remember black-and-white Rex, the dog we had the longest while I was at home. That Rex sometimes visited the dog across the railroad tracks, Shimniok's dog. One of those visits resulted in a litter of pups. About that same time Dad's brother, Richard, from Caledonia, Minnesota, needed a dog. Richard and Margaret drove the 100 miles and picked up one of the pups. When black and white Rex died, Richard's dog had just had pups. Richard and Margaret brought one to Mom and Dad. His name was Skipper. Soon after he arrived, Skipper took to leaving the lower farm to become a companion to our elderly neighbor, Julia Ellas. We never knew where Skipper went until after Julia died. Her husband, Roy, told Dad. Skipper never left the farm again.

37

Rabbits

Dad bumped into a rabbit nest one day while cutting hay, and rabbits scattered in all directions except for one little guy that he picked up and brought to the upper farm. He knew the bunny might die without attention. A dilapidated bushel basket was fashioned for a straw bed. We called it the little rabbit house. Mom decided to keep the rabbit house on the porch off the kitchen because spring evenings were still cool, and she knew the bunny was used to heat from its mama.

The door between the kitchen and porch was not closed once spring arrived. This kept the porch moderately warm and ventilated fresh spring air into our home. Mom figured the porch was warm enough for the baby rabbit, yet it would not actually be in her home. She used an eyedropper to feed the little guy at first. My brothers and I pulled fresh green grass every day that the rabbit soon nibbled to nothing. A short time later it was taking tiny hops around the rabbit house. When its hopping got higher and stronger, Dad laid the screened insert from our porch door on top of the rabbit house so the bunny could not hop out. We all knew the rabbit would be released, but he needed to be strong enough to survive on his own.

Mom was always awake early. One morning she found the screen knocked off the bushel basket. The rabbit house was empty, vacated. Mom was not happy—there was a rabbit on the loose in her house. The "sweet little bunny" instantly became "a rodent." Armed with a broom and our one and only flashlight, she peered into every corner and under every piece of furniture to find the critter. No luck. We went to bed with a rodent on the loose in our house.

Mom and Dad heard scratching during the night. They listened intently, then quietly got up and looked, but they could not find the bunny. The search continued into the third day. Mom fussed continually about that "damned rabbit."

She and Dad finally located the little guy in a corner of their bedroom, behind the chest of drawers. He was not so little anymore, and was much stronger. The rabbit was quick, but Dad was quicker. He used the broom to stabilize the bunny for the grab.

I watched as Dad carried the frantic rabbit outside by the scruff of its neck and released it into the clover field. That scratching and clawing animal, squirming to free itself, did not look like the same sweet little bunny we nursed in the bushel basket. We missed our pet but shed no tears. It was a relief. Mom settled down, and the rabbit was safely returned to its natural home.

Dad built a hutch when David and Allen each got a rabbit to raise as a pet, though we all knew we would eat them one day. The hutch was on the lawn southwest of the house in the shade of the elms beside the bridal wreath. It was only about three feet high and six feet long, with a separate compartment for each bunny. Each compartment had an opening to an outside pen enclosed with chicken wire.

My brothers sat in front of the hutch for hours and fed the bunnies individual blades of juicy grass or tasty clover from our lawn and fields. The boys hauled water and refreshed the straw bedding daily. The bunnies grew quickly, and lo and behold in short order, their pet rabbits had babies. Mom and Dad had no idea the rabbits they gave to my brothers were expecting babies.

"Yikes. This means trouble." Dad was somewhere between excited and worried.

"I don't want a whole bunch of rabbits in the backyard." Mom knew trouble was brewing. She was right because that first family of baby bunnies grew quickly. A much bigger hutch was needed, and fast.

David and Allen were spending a lot of time caring for their many rabbits. Dad bought bags of oatmeal-colored rabbit pellets because the bunnies required so much food; the boys could not keep up pulling grass to feed them. The hard extruded pellets were about the diameter of a thin pencil and cut into chunks about a half inch long.

An old makeshift shed behind the barn close to the outhouse on the upper farm became the rabbits' new home. Baby rabbits are cute, but they grow and reproduce very fast. David and Allen had almost a hundred rabbits when production peaked, which did not take long. The rabbits were of all varieties. Their colors ranged from snow-white to pitch-black, with many grays and browns; some were spotted, others dappled. The biggest rabbits weighed over 12 pounds; others never came close to that. The boys divided the shed with wide boards to separate adults from juveniles and babies. We butchered many rabbits that summer, and Mom served them as tasty meals just like the other meat from our farm.

When the rabbits occasionally escaped their home, I helped retrieve them. The field by the upper farm was planted with clover in the year of the rabbits. The clover was almost three feet tall when one pen of adults escaped. It was difficult to find the critters in the tall clover, especially the gray and brown ones. My technique was to stand still and look for movement of cloverleaves—approach very slowly hoping to catch the rabbit off guard as it devoured sweet blossoms—then pounce for the catch. Big rabbits were the easiest to spot, but strong and difficult to capture. White rabbits were easy to locate because when they jumped, their backs arched like a line of alabaster against the dark green clover. I remember David sneaking up and grabbing a huge white bunny. David was good at that. He caught the rabbit around its middle but could not lift it totally off the ground. With much effort, David dragged the struggling bunny back to the shed, its feet dangling behind.

Our family could only eat so much rabbit, and we were not about to go into the bunny business. The last of the rabbits were butchered in the fall. The animals had destroyed what was left of the old shed with their gnawing and waste. Dad knocked it down and hauled it to the burn pile after the rabbits were gone.

38

Cats, Mice, and Rats

There were always a bunch of cats on the lower farm. They scavenged for food and kept mice and other rodents at bay; snakes, too. We gave the cats fresh milk from our cows. They drank out of old pie tins and came running from all directions when the first drop of milk hit metal. When there were too many cats, Dad thinned the herd in ways that would be against the law today. We always had one cat at the upper farm, like the gray kitty with one foot missing because it had been caught in a trap. Like that cat, those at the upper farm were usually unique.

We inherited a white Angora. It had belonged to Elaine Tewes' mother; Elaine was married to Mom's cousin, Wally. That ball of fur was given to us when Elaine and her brothers gave their mother a bird for Christmas. The cat and bird did not get along with each other. I think the poor old lady did not want to give up her beautiful cat for the stupid bird. However, she knew her children would be upset if she gave away their gift, especially Elaine who probably came up with the bird idea.

The white cat stayed in our cellar. It was the only cat Mom ever officially permitted in the house. Mom felt it would not survive the cold because it had been an indoor cat. It was eventually allowed out of the cellar on rare occasions but was never allowed into the living room because of the never-used couch and the new green carpet.

In time, if the cellar door was not closed tightly the cat learned to put its paw under the door and pull it open. It was known to walk around Mom's legs while she was washing dishes. Mom pushed it away with her foot, but it immediately returned. That is when Mom began to call it "Doc," which stood for "Damn Old Cat."

One day, several years later, when I was in high school, we were sitting in the family room, the former dining room, watching television. We heard a sharp click and a loud cat screech. Doc had quietly wiggled open the cellar door, walked into the kitchen, entered the small pantry and tasted a dab of butter. Unfortunately for the cat, the butter was on a mousetrap. Doc got whapped on the nose.

This white ball of fur came flying from the kitchen into the family room like a blur. It headed for the living room, but frantically remembered the living room was off limits. Doc tried to stop by bracing with its front paws causing a long skid across the slippery linoleum. Its legs started pawing to the left midway through the skid.

We sat in a raised-up position as we watched Doc pawing toward the left with little traction before finally sliding into the frame of Mom and Dad's bedroom door with a soft bump. A streak of white headed to the cellar. We all had a good laugh before we thought to check the cat. There was a mark across its nose, but it had no other injuries. Doc rarely came upstairs uninvited again.

The white cat became quite a hunter and could eventually get in and out of the cellar through the crawl space under the kitchen. It went hunting and brought mice, snakes, and gophers back to the basement as trophies. Doc never ate them, only killed them and dragged them to the basement for us to remove.

One day Allen, now in the upper grades, was in the house alone and heard this terrible screeching. The noise came from the cellar so he went to investigate what was happening. There was Doc killing a wild baby rabbit by chewing on its neck. Allen did not like watching that awful scene, so he went outside until he thought the rabbit would be dead. He returned with a shovel, scooped the carcass and threw the dead bunny into the field. Doc watched this and looked at Allen as though proud of the gift it had given to him.

The Angora cat lived a pampered life before arriving at our farm, and trained us accordingly. Doc ate nothing but chicken necks. Mom had Pierce's Market in Baraboo save her 10 pounds of necks at a time. She wrapped them in packages of three and froze them. Every day we took a package out of the freezer for the cat's dinner.

One time at the grocery store, Mom put her total purchase of 10 pounds of chicken necks and a loaf of bread on the counter. After checking out, she stopped to put her pocketbook into her purse as the lady behind her leaned toward her. "If that's all you have to feed your family, I'll give you some of my hamburger." Mom chuckled and explained she needed only a loaf of bread at home on the farm; the chicken necks were for the cat, and she had five locker drawers full of meat. She also thanked the lady for being so thoughtful and generous. Both left the store with a smile.

Our cats were most effective for controlling the rodent population. The only mice I remember were an occasional mouse in the house in the fall of the year and a few in the cribs while sacking corn. They were a rare sight in the granary.

Allen talked about rats in the silo pits—they scared him. They multiplied when the pits were almost empty because they had nowhere to go. The pits were deep and the rats could not escape up the vertical walls. Allen climbed out of the pits a couple times and told Dad he was afraid of the rats. Hearing this, Dad went in and stabbed them with a fork, tossed them out and removed them. Allen said they were the most frightful things for him of all the farm work he did. After he told me, I was thankful I never had to be in the silo pits with rats.

The Forty

39

The Road to the Forty

We owned 40 acres of combination grassy pasture and shady woodland in the bluffs three-and-a-half miles south of the village. My grandparents, Louis and Hilda Kaun, bought this property from Bertha Krueger in 1944. My parents, Harold and Pearl Schroeder, bought it from my grandparents in 1958. Harold and Pearl Schroeder sold it to David and Patricia Schroeder in 1976. Of interest concerning the Forty, is that Timothy Hackett, Samuel and Dency's son, owned it in the late 1890s. Another connection between the two families. (Samuel and Dency Hackett were the original settlers of North Freedom.)

The gravel part of the Town of Freedom road to the Forty ended at the crest of the bluffs well before we arrived at the gate to the corral. A house stood at the end of the gravel road on Proverse's land; their family owned that property for years. Dad and Grandpa knew the Proverses, but I never saw them. There was a legal right of way for a road across the open field that the Town of Freedom offered to grade and gravel, but Mom and Dad refused because they did not want people going there.

We transported youngstock from the upper farm to the Forty in spring so we could clean the winter accumulation of manure from the small barn and adjacent yard. Also, the limited pasture behind the upper barn was not sufficient to feed our young cows all summer.

The herd of about twenty had to be checked, and their supply of water needed refreshing frequently. The cost made drilling a well in the rocky bluffs out of the question, so water was transported to the Forty in 10-gallon milk cans using our old International ton and half truck. It had a blue cab and a platform box with wooden sides that were painted red. Dad dug a small pond to collect runoff and rain, but the tank for the cows needed a regular replenish of fresh water. They were enticed to the corral with a serving of ground feed.

"Com'bos! Com'bos!" Dad called and banged pails together. It was not unusual for the youngstock to race to the corral for a taste of ground feed. They were often waiting for us when we arrived because the sound of the International crossing the field alerted them to our approach—and their treat. Dad dumped the 10-gallon pails of water from the back of the truck into the galvanized tank.

I was with Dad one warm summer day as the truck lumbered up the gravel road to the Proverse place. The corral gate was another half mile across the open rocky field and beyond. Two large rocks in our straightest path across the field were easily avoided in spring but were hidden in deep grass by early summer. Halfway across the field, Dad stopped the truck. "Find the pointed rock, Susie, and stand on it."

Tall grass tickled my shoulders, and buzzy black flies circled my sweaty head as I waved air to prevent them from landing on me. Fly bites left a bloody hole in your skin that hurt. I understood why cows constantly swished their tails to shoo away the bothersome insects. I stood tall on the rock, knowing from experience to stand where the side of the rock met the ground so Dad could judge exactly where to drive. When the truck was beside me, I hopped off the rock and into cab.

A short way beyond he stopped the truck again. "Find the flat one and stand on the north side." The flat rock was big around and surrounded by other rocks. Dad knew the tires of the truck had to be close to the north side of the flat rock to avoid ripping the bottom of the International.

Beyond the field, the last part of the road to the corral was a bumpy path between a stretch of trees. A big tree with thick branches close to the ground and another huge flat rock were just over the wooden fence at the corral. On special occasions, only a couple of times, Dad built a fire in the middle of that big stone, and the entire family roasted hotdogs and marshmallows for a picnic. My brothers and I enjoyed it so much we begged Mom to do it again. Mom however, was not much for picnics—or hauling food when we could eat at home.

I climbed the tree bouncing on its flexible low limbs while Dad worked with the youngstock. Sometimes he walked the perimeter of our land to check the fence. This took over an hour and became boring when I was alone. It was more fun when Dad brought all three of us kids to the Forty. It was then we each picked a big stone we pretended was a home where we lived. It was our own little village where we built stick buildings and invited our neighbors to parties.

Top: Carolyn's great aunt Martha (Beckman) Janzen, her maternal grandmother's sister, untangles yarn for Carolyn's sewing cards. *Bottom*: Carolyn's great aunt Emma Beckman, her maternal grandmother's sister, crochets as she sits in front of a radio console in her sister Martha's home.

40

Hickory Nuts

A grove of hickory nut trees was a short distance beyond the flat stone and the big tree at the Forty. It was a cool, damp autumn morning the first time I hauled a metal pail over the gate. Grandma Hilda and I were planning to pick up hickory nuts while Grandpa Louie checked the fence. I was five years old. We were wearing jackets and long pants; rubber boots protected our shoes from heavy dew. Grandma did not zip her boots because the stiff rubber cut at the calf of her leg. I was not allowed to mimic her actions; she was afraid I would trip and fall.

After picking for a while, I had to pee. This presented a dilemma I had not faced before. There was no bathroom. Grandma explained I would pee on the ground. I was not sure about that. We were out in the open after all. To solve the problem, she decided to demonstrate the procedure.

Under my watchful eye, Grandma, a tall slender lady with red frizzy hair above her faded freckled face, hiked her housedress, undid the warm long pants she wore underneath and held it all close to her chest as she squatted. She started to pee, then unsuccessfully tried to stop midstream when she realized – she was peeing into her gaping floppy boot.

"Darn it all." With her dress and pants gathered in front of her, she forgot her boots were unzipped. She was not happy as she collected herself. When our eyes caught, she suddenly remembered I was standing there and started to laugh.

"Hee! Hee! Hee!" Her high-pitched giggle drifted beyond the grove of hickory nut trees across the open pasture to the woods.

I laughed, too, because she looked really funny all bent and holding her pants and dress while balancing on one dry foot.

"Darn it all. I didn't want to do that." She hauled herself awkwardly to an upright position, pulling her long pants up and under her dress.

"Tee! Hee! Hee!" Her laughter tickled me.

"Ha! Ha! Ha!" Mine was a five-year old's belly laugh. I was bending over with tears in my eyes. "I need to pee really bad."

I completed my procedure successfully with little praise from Grandma. She was busy doing her best to dry her shoe and sock while her bare foot hung out in the cool fall air. I would remember this for a long time.

My grandparents and parents played cards with relatives on a regular basis, and the Sunday evening after the hickory nut episode was no exception. Martha and Emma, Grandma's sisters, along with other relatives, were at Grandma and Grandpa's house. Martha was tall and slender, and like Grandma, had red hair. Except Martha's was darker red with smooth curls. Emma looked like her sisters but was considerably shorter. My aunts doted on me, and I willingly contributed to their entertainment before card playing commenced. This particular evening, I politely listened to their conversation while anxiously waiting for Martha to ask what had happened since she last saw me.

"Carolyn, you are so grown up. What have you been doing lately?" I liked the way Martha talked directly to me. I lapped up the attention before I took a deep breath to tell my story.

"Grandma and I picked up hickory nuts at the Forty, and Grandma showed me how to go potty outside, and Grandma peed in her boot, and we laughed and laughed." I was breathless after holding my story inside waiting to be asked. Remembering how silly Grandma looked bent all killy whack, I laughed all over again. Initial chuckles erupted into hoots of laughter as I demonstrated Grandma's position.

The silliness was abruptly followed by stony silence as Grandma walked into the room. The pink on her neck turned rosy red on her cheeks. She was carrying Dad's favorite sunshine layer cake with burnt sugar frosting, topped with butternuts, on her stemmed cut glass serving plate. I was not sure what was happening. Grandma was not laughing like she did at the Forty. You could have heard a pin drop.

"Ha Ha Ha! Oh My! Ha Ha!" Grandma busted out loud and everyone joined her—relieved. I thought she must have really liked the way I told my story because I had never heard her laugh like that before.

41

LaRue

I rode along with Dad on many trips to the Forty. Counting cattle and filling the watering tank did not take long, and if no cows were missing, we were soon lumbering from the corral back to the gravel road. We did not go straight home those days; we stopped at Klingenmeyer's Bar on County Road PF. The place was operated by Wanda and Larry Klingenmeyer, who lived in the building and raised their six boys there. Their youngest son, Gary "Butch," was a year and a half older than me. The bar with adjoining dancehall was the last remnant of the once-thriving mining town of LaRue which was originally supported by the iron mines.

LaRue was founded by W. G. LaRue, a rock quarry owner from Minnesota, in 1903. He had stores, a church, and houses built for the many workers. LaRue had a population of over 500 in the early 1900s because of a boom in mining iron ore, but open pit mining in the Masabi Range in Minnesota forced the LaRue mines to close in 1914. Pumping water out of the mines made it too costly for the LaRue mines to compete.

The Rattlesnake Quarry owned by Harbison-Walker operated from 1917 through 1961. It opened because of a need for extra hard quartzite rock. This rock was shipped to

North Freedom

Indiana to be used to make firebrick to line blast furnaces. The mine employed about 40 men. I knew about the quarry because I overheard conversations between Mom and Dad and our neighbors, Elsie and Dan Worth. Dan worked at the quarry.

The surrounding rural population continued to support Klingenmeyer's Bar and dance hall after the quarry closed. The bar hosted area bands on weekends and card parties during the week. When Mom and Dad happened to be at some celebration at Klingenmeyer's and it got late, Wanda stacked tired youngsters on a bed in a room off the bar. On a few rare occasions I was in the stack.

Dad capitalized on the opportunity to stop at Klingenmeyer's Bar for a shot and a beer, a cigarette, and a candy bar. His short dark hair curled around his neck and from under his straw hat as he sat on a bar stool in his striped overalls exchanging stories and jokes with Larry and the other patrons. Wanda was usually in the kitchen, located just off the bar, but popped out to say hello to Dad and me.

By the time I was eight years old, Dad would let me have a sip of his shot if he was drinking blackberry brandy. He would also buy a vanilla Bun candy bar for me; he liked the maple nut flavor better.

Dad preferred stopping at Klingenmeyer's rather than the bars in North Freedom because Mom was less likely to hear about it. There was a good chance one of our neighbors might mention to Mom they saw Schroeder's truck parked uptown if he went to one the bars in the village. Dad did not relish explaining these kinds of situations to Mom, who did not drink alcohol.

42

Grandpa and the Man

Grandpa Louie took turns with Dad checking the Forty. One fall day he saw a car parked across from the house on the Proverse land where the gravel road ended. The car did not look familiar and there was no one around. "What is the car doing there? Who was driving it?" He scratched his head, then mulled the puzzle as he drove across the field and along the stretch of trees.

Grandpa had planned to count the cows then pick up a pail of hickory nuts. The past couple days he had been thinking about cracking nuts on the piece of log turned upright in the basement of their new home; he and Grandma Hilda had recently moved from the lower farm into a house on Franklin Street in the village. Crack. Crack. Crack. That pleasant thought was now interrupted because of the strange car. He stopped at the corral and climbed the gate.

What? There were people by the grove of hickory nut trees.

"Hey you, what're you doing?" Grandpa hollered as he approached.

"Get out of here! Who are you?" the man thundered back.

"What do you think you're doing?" Grandpa growled, his face turning red.

The fellow, his wife, and a couple of kids were picking up our hickory nuts.

"You better leave. We have permission to pick these nuts. I'll tell Louis Kaun. He owns this land." The man roared with authority.

"I'm Louie Kaun. By thunder, I own this property and have never given you or anyone else permission to walk on my land. And, you do not have permission to help yourself to my hickory nuts." Grandpa's voice dropped an octave to a threatening snarl.

Before Grandpa was done hollering, the lady and children were already skedaddling over the corral gate. The man's eyes darted around. He grunted, picked up his pail and walked away.

"Those are my hickory nuts, by thunder. Give'm here." Grandpa closed in and scooped every last nut from the pail the stranger was still holding.

The man slunk away and never came back as far as we knew.

Church

St. Paul's Lutheran Church, North Freedom, Wisconsin, circa 1950s.
(Photograph contributed by Louise Vater Crisman)

43

The Lady

There were three churches in North Freedom: Lutheran, Methodist, and Baptist. We were Lutheran. We went to church and Sunday school every week unless we were sick. The best time at church was Christmas Eve because the Sunday School children held a program. There were Bible verses or pieces of Christmas narrative to memorize and songs to learn by heart.

We all wore our best clothes. I hitched up my warm white stockings to my garter belt instead of the usual, everyday brown ones. The church was full of people all the way to the front. My grandparents and great aunts, Martha and Emma, were there; sometimes even more relatives came. Each child got a hefty bag of candy, peanuts, an apple and an orange. After the program the whole family went to our house, and we opened presents.

Every year Dad told us he and his ten brothers each got an orange for Christmas. He said it was the greatest thing. He was born in 1912 in Caledonia, Minnesota, and was the second youngest in the family. I wondered how his parents managed to provide an orange for each of those boys during the winter.

My brothers and I knew Christmas was coming soon when we saw Christmas tree lights appearing in windows along Walnut Street. Then the first string of colorful lights appeared across the street uptown, followed later by a second string. This added to our excitement. Finally, the biggest Christmas tree we ever saw stood glowing majestically next to the Gothic altar at our church.

My favorite part of church was the hymns, watching the coordination between melodies I heard and notes I saw. Reading the words improved my vocabulary. I taught myself to play favorite hymns after taking a few piano lessons when I was nine years old. When my brother Allen learned to play them, I sang. I was best at the alto part because my voice got all squeaky when the melody was high.

My early memories were of ushers holding a big stack of hymnals, religious songbooks, used for the singing part of the church service. These heavy blue books were lined along one of their arms hooked at the bottom with their fingertips. They handed these to folks who did not bring a personal hymnal to church. Many members had confirmation hymnals they had received as gifts. Church members often donated these religious songbooks for special occasions or as memorials; each donation or memorial was noted inside the front covers. After a number of hymnals were donated to the church, the books were placed in the slatted wooden racks on the back of each pew, and the handing out stopped.

A number of hymnals had Badger Lutheran Church noted inside. Those had been used at the church at Badger Village twelve miles southeast of North Freedom. That village, including the church building, had been constructed in 1942 by the government to house people employed at Badger Ordnance Works, later renamed Badger Army

Ammunition Plant. The plant manufactured gunpowder for the US Army and was locally referred to as the powder plant.

Badger Village was built directly across Highway 12 from the main entrance of the plant so employees could walk to work from this quasi city during World War II. Tires and gasoline were rationed, making owning a car and driving a luxury or impossible. At the end of the war in September 1945, the plant abruptly closed. Employees living at Badger Village moved elsewhere looking for work. The church closed, and some of the Badger hymnals ended up at our Lutheran church.

We were expected to sit quietly and participate during church services. On those occasions when my brothers and I were too restless or noisy in church, a poke from Mom quickly and firmly reminded us to straighten up.

We knew everyone in the congregation, some only by their unique appearance. Men wore dress shirts and ties; some wore suits. Ladies dressed up. Many wore hats, some with veils. A few of the veils hung low over ladies' eyes creating a dramatic effect. When I was twelve years old, I had a hot pink pillbox hat with a short little brim and a piece of pink netting wrapped around the crown. It had no veil. Mom had several hats; hers were small and conservative.

One tiny older lady wore a navy blue hat with a medium length veil that fell just below her eyes. She used bobby pins to secure it to her fuzzy short gray hair. One day she came to church with the veil stretched down and tucked under her nose. The veil was not quite long enough for that, so the tip of her nose was slightly pulled upward, making her nostrils overly predominate on her otherwise small face. The force of the veil hooked on her nose tugged up her fuzzy gray hair in the back. This exposed transparent white skin where she had shoved extra bobby pins to secure the hat in place. She walked in all proper and sat down in the pew in front of us.

I thought her effort to look dramatic was not working. I glanced at Allen. We lost it! We giggled noiselessly until tears rolled down our cheeks.

Poke! Poke! "Straighten up."

One hot humid Sunday in August, I was sitting next to Allen. Everyone was sweating. Ladies were using the personal hand fans that had been placed in the hymnal racks, compliments of area funeral homes. All of the bottom sections of the stained glass windows were wide open, as was the front door of the church.

Before the end of the second hymn, Allen and I noticed the flies: big, black end-of-summer flies. As flies landed on different people, it became funny to Allen and me. One fly was particularly persistent. It would land on a shoulder. Swish! It would land on an ear. Swish! It would land on a bald spot, on David, on Mom. Swish! Swish! Swish! The fly was hilarious.

Buzzzzz! The fly had been swished, startled and flew like a slingshot projectile between Allen and me. We simultaneously caught a quick glance where it went as it flew behind us.

There we saw that old lady with the navy blue hat with the veil tucked under her pulled up nose, and that fly had somehow managed to get under the veil. She was swatting and blinking like crazy. We snapped back and sat at attention facing the altar.

Tears and sweat rolled down our faces.

Poke! Poke! "Straighten up."

We tried, but it was not possible. I saw my stomach jiggling up and down as I stifled laughter that managed to slip out between my pursed lips. Allen snorted through his nose as tears dripped off his chin. The flies continued to buzz.

Mom's face was turning red. Was it the heat or did her children embarrass her? Allen and I thought we saw her cheeks crinkle. Did she know what we were laughing about?

Top: St. Paul's Lutheran Church interior, 1986. The interior looks much as it did in the 1950s. *Bottom*: Carolyn, Allen, and David open Christmas presents after the Christmas Eve church service in 1954. Grandma Hilda sewed their clothes for this special event.

44

Offerings

My first allowance was a nickel a day during the week. I remember the amount because I could buy a candy bar for a nickel at Gehrmann's grocery store uptown, one for each weekday. Or, I could save five nickels and capitalize on Gehrmann's special offer of six candy bars for a quarter. It was not easy to wait until I had twenty-five cents, but I usually did. My favorites were Hershey's plain chocolate or Mounds bars because they were good sized and easily divided to last two days. Joe and Florence were the proprietors. Florence was usually at the cash register, but sometimes their son, Jim, took over.

I did not get an allowance on Saturday and Sunday. That money was given to the church. Every Sunday before church, Mom pressed a dime into my hand, my brother's hands too. We were told to put the dimes inside our mittens during winter so we would not drop the small, slippery coins in the snow.

During summer I often wore white gloves to church, like the other girls. It was not unusual for my dime to get stuck in one of the fingers of a white glove. This was even more problematic when I was old enough to wear long white gloves that came up toward my elbows. Sometimes

I was still fiddling with my glove, trying to dislodge my dime when the collection plate arrived in front of me. The usher would not so patiently wait, while Mom was poking me to hurry along.

When I started babysitting, it was a bit of a shock that Mom quit handing out allowance to me. I guess she thought my babysitting money was enough income for an eleven-year-old. However, Mom supplemented my church offerings until I was in high school.

45

Pump Organs

I took piano lessons for six months from Mrs. Waddell out by Seeley Lake when I was nine years old. Those lessons were not as intimidating as they might have been since I knew this talented lady before Mom first dropped me at her home. Her son, Rollie, was my classmate.

Mrs. Waddell was an exceptionally pleasant person with a sweet smile. However, sometimes her expectations of my piano playing exceeded my talent. This was primarily due to the way I practiced. I played pieces I liked repetitively and avoided challenging melodies. Within a few weeks, I was entertaining my family.

After each piano lesson, I taught my brother Allen what I had learned. He was like a sponge and later became much more proficient than me at both piano and organ. Allen would say I was better at sight reading; and he played a lot by memorization. He eventually played for chapel at seminary as he trained for the ministry. I could take credit for passing along the only music lessons Allen ever had, but I came to realize he probably would have taught himself to play without me. My lessons ended after six months because Mom needed me at home. My brother, Randy, was a baby. He was sick a lot.

Our church was small; sometimes we shared a pastor with another church. There was a kitchen and fellowship room in the basement where two pump organs were pushed against the walls. The bellows inside these organs were filled with air by continuously pumping the foot pedals while you played. They were also called "reed organs" because air from the bellows blowing across metal reeds made the sound.

One of the organs was pretty well worn out. In the early 1950s, the Ladies' Aid wanted it removed from the basement and referred this project to the church council. After much discussion, council found no one wanted the old thing, and it would cost money to haul it away. Dad, who was on the council, said he would take it home and store it in our new garage at the upper farm. Council thought that was a wonderful idea.

Grandpa scowled. "I ain't a'gonna help haul the damn thing. They'll just want it back." He did not help.

Mom was none too pleased, either. The Ladies' Aid had been in her craw for a while, starting back with the first disagreement Grandpa Louie had with the church. "Those women should find a better way to use their time than to sit at meetings discussing how the church should be run."

Dad was not happy either, after hearing this criticism of his good deed. Without Grandpa's assistance, and my brothers too young to help, Dad was stuck. He finally paid a couple of our regular hired men to drag the organ across the fellowship hall and hoist it up the steep stairwell out of the basement and onto our truck. He hauled the old pump organ home, and the men helped move it into our garage.

This was no easy task. The Lutherans had added the basement after they bought the church building from the Baptists, evidently through the Hirschingers, a family from

Baraboo who belonged to a Methodist church there. (Our family was never sure how the Hirschingers came to own our church property in North Freedom.) The narrow cement stairwell with a sharp corner at the bottom was the only egress to remove the organ.

The ladies were empowered by the success of achieving their goal, and the size of the group grew. Later on, when the infamous Ladies' Aid usurped all power over the church basement as their domain, they decided the second pump organ, since it was unused and an eyesore, had to go. The Sunday School never used it because they practiced music in the church. It was loud when played and disrupted classes, meetings or other activities happening elsewhere in the small building. Additionally, removing the pump organ from the basement would give them more room for serving food and seating people, and—"It removed the temptation for children to play it." This comment was made by one of the ladies as she gave me a piercing look.

No one wanted this pump organ either. Reluctantly, but being the congenial man he was, Dad offered to store the second organ in our garage. He had not consulted with Mom.

"Those old biddies see our new garage, and they think we should store their stuff. If the church doesn't want the organ, they should sell it or throw it out. It's not right." Mom's face turned red every time she thought about the two organs in our garage.

In the meantime, Dad once again enlisted help to haul the second organ out of the church basement and bring it home. He put it in the garage along with the first.

With permission, David and Allen took the dilapidated pump organ apart. My brothers and I played the reeds like a giant harmonica.

North Freedom

Dad remembered Grandpa's comment. He sat us down and told us we had to take good care of the better organ. It belonged to the church, and they might want it back. After Dad's talk I dusted that pump organ every Saturday, just like the furniture in the house. It shined like it never had when it was in the church basement.

The better organ sat in our garage for several years. For fun, David, Allen and I pulled everything out of the two-stall garage and clamped on metal roller skates. Allen and I took turns pumping and playing music while we whizzed around the cement floor to waltzes, polkas and hymns.

Several years later there was a question at church as to what happened to the pump organ that had been in the basement. Dad said it was in our garage.

One member of the Ladies' Aid suggested it was the church's organ and wondered what it was doing in Schroeder's garage. Several other ladies raised their eyebrows and stared at Dad.

Unruffled, Dad calmly explained how the organ came to be in our garage.

It did not make any difference what Dad said. The ladies wanted it back.

Mom hit the roof. "I told you they'd want it back! Those old bats, who do they think they are? What are they going to do with the organ now that they couldn't do with it before?"

Grandpa snickered as he watched from the barn door. I think Grandpa had gone through a similar experience with the Ladies' Aid years earlier and figured Dad had to learn the same lesson. Again, he did not help.

Dad did not say any more about hauling the organ back to church. My brothers were now strong enough to help drag it out of the garage, onto the truck, unload it, and inch it down the sunken cement staircase, around the sharp corner and back into the fellowship hall.

Shortly thereafter, that pump organ disappeared from the church basement never to be seen again. Until . . .

When my brother David and his wife moved into the house in front of Uncle Louie's shed house on Lieder Street in 1966, lo and behold, that pump organ was in the basement of that house—and the man who owned the house was not a member of our church. No one could explain how it got there.

Mom was livid. "Evidently the Ladies Aid didn't really want that organ. They just didn't want us to have it." Mom attended church services regularly and made many dishes for the meals served there, but she was never a member of the Ladies' Aid.

The organ never returned to the church basement.

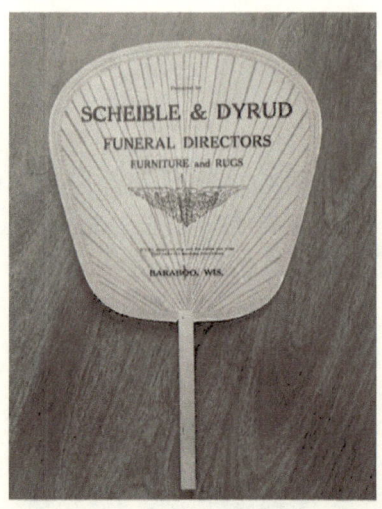

Top: A fan from St. Paul's Lutheran Church. Area funeral homes donated these fans to churches to advertise their business. *Bottom*: Rose Myers cuts cookie bars in the kitchen of St. Paul's Lutheran Church during the 1970s. (Photos contributed by Carolyn Myers Blum.)

46

Funeral

There had been a huge pipe organ in the St. Paul's Lutheran Church balcony that was replaced in the 1950s with an electronic organ. The pipe organ was actually rather small as pipe organs go, but it filled most of the balcony of the small church; everything seemed bigger when I was a child. Marie Gurgel, our organist, was short, hardly five feet tall. Her back was to the altar when she played; she perched on pillows and needed a mirror to see pastor's directions at the front of the church.

    Mom did not want our family to sit in the church balcony. She thought kids fooled around up there and did not pay attention. I wanted to go to the balcony because of the organ. Sometimes, on special Sundays when Grandpa came to our church, he took me up the narrow stairway to where the steps were skinny triangles at the sharp turn at the top, and the ceiling so low that adults had to stoop to turn the corner.

    I did not fool around in the balcony. I watched Marie's graceful hands move across the double keyboard. Her fingers were short, but she somehow managed to hit all the keys with perfect timing. The foot pedals had been adjusted to accommodate Marie's small stature.

It was good that Marie could play the organ, because she had health issues, and her physical abilities were limited. She lived with her parents, Otto and Meta. After they died, her sister Josephine cared for her. My brothers and I thought her mother's name was funny. We giggled every time we heard it, and we heard it often enough because Meta Gurgel was active in the Ladies' Aid.

The Gurgel family lived on Walnut Street close to uptown and had a huge garden with attractive colorful flowers along the sidewalk. I went past their place all year and could tell the seasons by what was blooming in Meta's garden. She, and later Josephine, brought fresh cut flowers to decorate the church.

"The bellows were originally pumped by hand." Grandpa liked to explain things he thought I should know. He pointed out the pump handles coming from the side of the organ. I could not see the bellows, but Grandpa described how they worked inside, by blowing air through the pipes. I had not known that sometimes it took two people, a pumper and a player, to make music.

"Later an electric motor was added to work the bellows. After that, one of the ushers could turn on the motor, and Marie could play without the help of a pumper." Grandpa took particular pride and pleasure in telling this story; so much so that I wondered if he was involved in this revolutionary change.

Marie stopped playing about the same time the church got rid of the pipe organ. Getting rid of the pipe organ was a bad mistake because any pipe organ can be repaired and last for another fifty to one hundred years or more. People in our church were probably not aware of this, and they did not research the possibilities. My hunch is they assumed the pipe organ, like the pump organs, was junk because they were all old.

We heard it went to a farmer southwest of town, and we are quite sure it was given away so the church did not have to pay for it to be hauled. The church most likely never thought to charge for the pipe organ and was glad someone took it at the time.

The new electronic organ was a Kimball. It had a long belt that made a full sweep around the back. The belt was hidden behind a wooden panel. On a hot day, the belt expanded causing the sound to wobble. To fix this problem, Oscar Baumgarten, one of our church members, had to remove the wooden panel, kneel at the backside of the organ, and put pressure on the belt with the side of a screwdriver to keep it taut and the sound steady. Oscar and his family lived next to the church; he served in many capacities over the years.

I was starting my freshman year of high school when the church council talked to my parents. The current organist, Pastor Hertler's wife, was in the hospital for emergency surgery. She would be incapacitated for an extended period of time. "Would Carolyn play the organ on Sunday?"

"Yes." Mom and Dad said I would play—then they told me.

"Why did you do that? Why did you say I would?" I was horrified. How could I do it? All those notes I didn't know. Those foot pedals. All those people.

"What if I make a mistake? I've only had six months of piano lessons when I was nine years old. Why did you say I would play?"

They listened to me wail before they explained. "You are the only person in our church who has had music lessons. Everyone will understand you need time to learn the music."

"Yah, right."

Also Mrs. Stackman, a well-known organist from Rock Springs, three miles to the west, would teach me preludes, postludes and the liturgy, the regular opening and closing of the church service. I would have a key to the church so I could practice on their organ whenever I wanted. I would be paid four dollars each Sunday. The church would pay Mrs. Stackman for my lessons and associated music.

"Four dollars each Sunday." The number echoed through my mind. It was 1961. My regular babysitting job for seven children paid 25 cents an hour before midnight and 50 cents an hour after midnight. I was a freshman in high school.

"Four dollars. Four dollars."

"I could do it."

That Sunday pastor announced what had happened. I would play a single note melody as I learned the music needed for the church service. The congregation was to sing loudly to help me.

I worked long and hard to learn the liturgy. Additionally, pastor selected four hymns to be sung each Sunday. This compounded my work exponentially. There were 660 hymns printed in our hymnals. We hardly ever sang the same ones twice during the church year. Pastor seemed surprised when I told him, "I need the list of Sunday hymns by Wednesday so I can practice. I'll ask you to try again if one is too challenging."

Just as my confidence was building, there was a funeral. Reuben, one of the Blackmun brothers, died. Three siblings lived in North Freedom, two men and a woman. They could not hear or speak. A different pastor from the seminary would perform the service. It would be presented in sign language.

I was surprised to learn a significant number of strangers would attend the service. These folks were not friends or relatives of Reuben Blackmun. They were people from south central Wisconsin that could read, or were interested in, sign language. Some could not hear. Several came from a place folks called the County Farm on the other side of Rock Springs. Some of those people were staff members; others were residents.

The Sauk County Farm was a facility where folks went when there was no one to care for them or take care of their needs. These folks came to Reuben's service for the signing experience, a rare opportunity in our rural area. They used every chance to see the spoken word, even a funeral for someone they did not know.

The signing pastor explained to me how the service would progress. "I will speak and sign the service simultaneously. However, the hymns will be signed much faster than sung by the singing people." He would not wait for the organ and the singing folks to finish. I was to continue playing the whole hymn for the singing people while he began talking.

True to his word, that pastor started speaking and signing away right in the middle of the first hymn. Startled by the interruption in the middle of their song, the singing folks pretty much quit singing as soon as he started speaking.

What should I do? Without thinking, I increased the volume and played on. I figured if I had to finish, so did they. The singers took the hint and joined the organ.

Ed Steinhorst pulled the rope to toll the bell as I played a solemn postlude at the end of Reuben's service. I was never that close to a tolling bell before. The empty balcony vibrated from the friction of the rope between the entryway where Ed stood, and the slow thunderous strikes of the heavy bell in the steeple. I had heard tolling for other funerals from home as the bell rang once for each year of the deceased's life, like a faraway mournful closure. The tolling bell the day of Rueben Blackmun's funeral was a jarring ominous sound I will never forget.

Most bell ringing was a joyous calling of people to worship. Ed rang the bell every Saturday evening at six o'clock to signal that the week's work was finished, and it was time to prepare hearts and minds for Sunday worship. The few times Ed was not available, one of the ushers rang the bell. If an inexperienced bell ringer was short in stature, the momentum of the bell could lift him several feet off the floor until he got the hang of controlling it.

Ten organ lessons with Mrs. Stackman averaged almost three hours each. I improved and gained confidence but relied on those fun technical features of the electric organ to augment actual musical skill and ability. For the most part, my playing sounded good but was technically lacking. There was always a bit of oom-pah-pah in the hymns.

47

A Mystery

We did not have an organ at home so I practiced at church after school and on Saturdays. About eight to ten church members made up our small choir before I starting playing. By late fall the choir wanted to sing for Christmas. This meant learning more music and scheduling practices. My salary did not increase. Music had to be accurate and technically correct for the choir. I did not want to discourage current choir members or prevent the few potential new members from joining.

It was dusk most school nights by the time I entered the church and climbed the narrow stairs to the balcony that first fall. It was during one of those practices I heard muffled talking. Working intently, I must not have heard the church doors open so I played on. A while later, I distinctly heard talking again. There was definitely someone in the church. What were they saying? I stopped playing abruptly and listened. I heard nothing.

"Hello!" No answer. "Hello?" They must have left. I played on. Voices again. Stop.

"Hello!" Nothing. This is silly. It is certainly not nice to mess with the organist.

The nave, the main part of the small church, and the sanctuary and the altar were dark; only the balcony, the narthex and the entry were lighted. I left the organ turned on and crossed the balcony to the top of the curved stairway as I watched below for someone to move. I glanced down as my foot dropped to the first narrow triangular step. Quietly I descended to the main floor.

"Hello?" Nothing. I stepped through the swinging doors leading into the narthex and pushed the button, illuminating the main seating area and the altar.

"Hello. Who's there? I'm the organist, Carolyn. Who's there?" Still nothing.

I stood perfectly still. Surely, I would hear someone moving.

"This is not good." Mustering courage, I turned slowly and cautiously then climbed the narrow passage back to the balcony not taking my eyes off the interior of the church.

"Come on, move. I know you're here." Nothing. I crossed the creaky wooden balcony floor and turned the organ off. Its low hum stopped.

My eyes stayed on the front of the church as I felt my way into the sleeves of my warm coat. The floor creaked again as I crossed to the stairs and stepped down to the main floor by the front door. My hand hesitated as I reached for the light button and stopped.

With a turn, I silently opened the front door expecting to catch the intruder. It was quiet outside and dark, except for the dim streetlight. Soft snow was falling. There were no tracks around the front of the church.

"They must have left through the side door by the altar or from the basement." I reached back, pushed the light off and scurried outside.

Slip sliding the short block to Walnut Street in the dim light, I glanced over my shoulder, fearing someone, or something, was following me. Turning east, my pace slowed as I continued the four blocks home.

Mom was expecting me to start supper. Dad and the boys were still at the lower farm because chores took longer with winter approaching.

"Mom, there was somebody in the church while I was practicing."

"Oh really. Who was there?"

"I didn't see anyone. I just heard them."

"What did they say?"

"I couldn't understand them. I listened a couple times."

"What did they look like?"

"I don't know. I said I didn't see them." She was not even listening to me.

"Were they in the basement?"

"Maybe. It didn't sound that way."

My story was diluted now that I was home, slicing boiled potatoes for frying and thinking about algebra homework. Maybe there was not anyone in the church after all—but maybe there was.

I brought the matter up again at the supper table. "Dad, there was somebody talking in the church while I practiced."

"Who was it?"

"I don't know. I turned on all the lights. I looked for them. It was scary."

"What were they talking about?"

"I couldn't understand them."

"What did you do?"

"I turned on all the lights and looked around. I called out a couple times. I asked who was there. I said I was Carolyn, the organist. No one answered."

I saw the quick glance between Mom and Dad.

"Well Susie, finish up and we'll go to church." Dad always called me Susie. It was short for "Susie Q," the popular song.

Wow. This was serious. I did not think they would believe me.

Dad and I drove to church and parked in the glow of the streetlight. He suggested we look around before we got out of the car. He did not want evidence of visitors to the church disturbed.

There were a few tracks through the newly fallen snow on the sidewalk, but none on the steps to the front door of the church or on either side of the small building. I felt important as I turned the key and let Dad inside and pushed on the lights—nothing. We checked the small rooms on each side of the altar—nothing. Nothing in the basement. Nothing in the balcony.

"Well Susie, you heard something, but there's nothing here. Maybe someone was talking outside."

Maybe so, maybe that is what I heard.

"I did hear people talking."

"I know you did, Susie. Let's go home."

I was cautious as I walked into church the following evening, up the stairs and across the balcony. I turned the organ on. I had turned on all the lights in the main level. Night after night I practiced music for the Christmas program. I loved the simple old songs the children would sing. I worked to perfect the choir's music.

A couple weeks later I heard voices, distant voices—again. I stopped playing. Nothing! Play! Voices! Stop! Nothing!

Play! Voices! Stop! Nothing! What were they talking about? What were they planning? Did it involve me? I pedaled the organ volume down and played on, trying to listen. The voices came and went. Short. Choppy. No emotion. Like military signals. The powder plant? Could it be?

"Hello! Hello?" Nothing. Again, I left and walked home in the snow beneath the soft glow of streetlights.

I had to bring it up at the supper table. "I heard the voices again. They were talking in the church."

"What did they say?" Dad eyes turned to me.

"I couldn't understand them. I quit playing to listen, and they quit talking. I played soft and loud. I could hear them, but they stopped talking every time I stopped playing."

I had not felt scared until I saw the glance between Mom and Dad. They did not believe me. My stomach did an unsettled flip-flop.

After dinner when we were alone, Dad asked, "Susie, are you afraid to practice in the church?"

"No. I just don't like to hear the voices."

"Well, Mom and I cannot come to the church with you. We would like you to keep playing the organ. Is that okay?"

"Yes." I would keep playing. I would not quit because someone was trying to scare me. I had learned a lot. I liked playing.

The next time I heard the voices, I listened intently. Where were they coming from? I did not call out. Play! Voices! Stop! Play! Voices! Stop! Volume pedal up. Volume pedal down. Play! Voices! Stop!

The voices were coming from the organ! Over and over again I could make the voices talk, and I could make them stop. I could hear them, but I could not make out what was being said.

I could hardly wait until supper to tell Mom and Dad about my discovery.

"I heard the voices again. They're coming from the organ."

Glances darted across the kitchen table. Mom glanced at Dad. Dad glanced at Mom. Mom and Dad glanced at me.

"Well Susie. Let's go to church."

I hurried up the steps and through the front door, anxious to demonstrate for Dad how I could manipulate the voices. I raced to the balcony. Dad was not far behind. I played a few bars. A few more. A whole song. I played softly. I played loud. As many times as I tried to make the voices talk for Dad, they said nothing.

Before bed Mom was serious. "We cannot sit with you at church. If you don't see anyone just keep playing."

"Okay." My eyes hardened; my jaw set. That is exactly what I had planned to do. I would figure out the voices myself.

The choir was strong and carried my accompaniment. Oscar Baumgarten, now the congregation's president, sang; his deep voice was solid and unwavering. It was mid-December, and the group was fine-tuning dynamics for their Christmas Eve piece when, spontaneously—I heard the voices. I stopped playing right in the middle of their singing. There was nothing. Nothing?

"Did you hear voices?"

"No." The choir was emphatic. I felt my face turning red. These adults were leading members of our congregation and of our community. I was only 14 years old. They did not hear the voices. I was shaken. My hands trembled slightly over the keys as I resumed playing.

Voices! Stop!

"I hear voices coming from the organ." These people must hear them.

"Let me over there." Oscar's bass voice matched his size. He rounded the front of the narrow pew towards my perch on the organ bench and stooped to the main speaker by my knees. Nothing! Oscar was beginning to heft himself upright when I heard it.

"I hear voices." I pushed the volume pedal. His eyes popped wide. He heard it too.

"What the ...," Oscar boomed.

Choir rehearsal continued as though nothing had happened.

I was not privy to the investigation. Adults did not think children should be involved in these matters. I was miffed because I was excluded. I discovered the voices. I had continued to point adults toward the problem even when they did not believe me.

The explanation was that one of the older boys in the village had a hobby of operating a HAM radio located near our church. When he was transmitting, a strong AM radio signal was received at the organ from the nearby HAM radio transmitter. The organ functioned as a radio receiver tuned to the same frequency as that being transmitted by the neighboring HAM operator. When conversing with a fellow HAM, they alternated between transmitting and listening.

It is fortunate that Oscar was listening to the "organ radio receiver" at exactly the same time the neighboring HAM operator was talking while transmitting. Who knows how long, if ever, someone else would have heard voices coming from the organ besides me.

I suspect that when informed of the situation, the HAM radio operator tuned his transmitter to avoid operating at the same frequency to which the organ radio receiver was tuned, thereby avoiding interference with the organ. In any event, I never heard those voices again.

I was organist at St. Paul's Lutheran Church in North Freedom during all four years of high school. I missed only one Sunday; I had measles.

I wanted my own organ. Mom and Dad did not have that kind of money. Determined, and with the money I received for playing at church and babysitting, over the course of a year and a half, I bought a small electric Magnavox organ from Kirchstein Electronics in Prairie du Sac, a few miles beyond the powder plant. I was able to upgrade to a larger Wurlitzer organ before I graduated from high school.

48

Roller Skating

There was a roller skating rink in the new community center at Rock Springs, three miles west of North Freedom; Sunday evening was open skating. The history of the building was mentioned in a statement made by Flood Recovery Chairman, Jamie Busser, quoted in the Reedsburg Times-Press, April 2, 2019, as follows: "The 60 X 120 foot community center is a 'working person building' since the village's everyday people helped construct the building ... it was constructed in the late 1940s with land and material donated by the village, the Town of Freedom, the Town of Westfield and the Town of Reedsburg." This statement was made after the 2018 flood damaged the building along with the rest of downtown Rock Springs; everything was beyond saving. (As of this writing, the village is moving the downtown district to higher ground out of the flood plain.)

Mom drove us to the rink occasionally as a special treat. We rented lace-up shoe skates that were much nicer than the metal ones we clamped to our shoes with a key when we skated in our garage. The rink was managed by a man named Harold Schneider, who also drove bus for the Reedsburg School District. He was known as Chully. There was a large wooden floor for skating, and a stage where a Hammond organ sat. I loved Hammond organs because they had slides that added pleasing dynamics to melodies with little extra effort from the organist. Mrs. Stackman, the woman who gave lessons to me, had a Hammond. Diane Woelfl, an accomplished organist, who was a year behind me in school, played the organ for skating.

After I received my driver's license, Mom no longer needed to drive us back and forth to skate. Our only car, a lavender and white Plymouth sedan, was somehow always available Sunday evenings for me to take my brothers and several youngsters I babysat to the rink.

Chully skated over to me one night. "I understand you play the organ."

"Yes. I play at St. Paul's Lutheran Church in North Freedom."

"Would you be interested in playing here at the rink?" he asked. "Diane would like a chance to skate. I would need you to play for about a half hour or so while she takes a break. I can't pay you, but you could skate for free. I wouldn't charge you admission or skate rental."

Wow! I would get to play the Hammond organ! On stage! I felt like a movie star just thinking about it. There was no practice time; I started cold turkey and pretty much played the same songs each week, although my repertoire expanded over the next couple years. I eventually married one of the skate boys.

As a teenager, I noticed many of the other skaters my age had their own skates. The girls made fluffy colorful pompoms out of yarn and attached them to the front of their feet by tying them to the laces over their toes. It was not unusual for these girls to make color coordinated pom-poms for their boyfriends.

I wanted my own skates. I was earning money as church organist and babysat for the family next door. They had five children when they moved in and soon added two more. The parents frequently played cards a couple nights every week uptown or at LaRue. I earned 25 cents an hour before midnight and 50 cents an hour after midnight. A basic pair of skates cost over 25 dollars without a case. I knew it would be a long time before I had enough money to buy a new pair of roller skates.

Mom and Dad knew my dilemma. They suggested I use the Doboy coupons that came with special farm products to get a pair of skates. Bender's Feed Mill uptown carried Doboy products that Dad used on the farm. These three-by-five-inch coupons were stitched to the top of bags containing special animal feed. Only the narrow strip on the edge of the coupon was needed for redemption. I had watched Mom cut these coupons and redeem them for small kitchen appliances, pans, dishes and silverware.

When Mom handed the Doboy catalog to me, a slip of paper marked the page showing roller skates. I cannot remember exactly how many coupons I needed; it was in the hundreds. I cut the strips and bundled them into bunches of 25 with rubber bands. I collected these coupons for months. My stash of bundles was kept in a cigar box that eventually lost the smell of cigars and wafted the smell of cow feed. Carefully following their instructions, I mailed the box of coupons to the Doboy people.

When I received my package in the mail, the aroma hinted at what was in the box. I anxiously pulled away packing to reveal beautiful white leather shoe skates with light-colored wooden wheels. I continued saving coupons, and in a relatively short time, a maroon and white metal case held my skates. I still have them, although the skate boy, my husband, replaced the wooden wheels with new ones made of a composite material that better gripped wooden floors. We could waltz, two step, conga and limbo on roller skates.

One crisp winter evening, my charges scrambled into the car after skating. The temperature had warmed during the day and heavy fog now hung low over snow and frozen ground. There was no breeze. I followed two cars over the railroad tracks, past the feed mill and headed east out of Rock Springs toward home. The cars ahead of me continued their slow pace going down the hill into the dark agricultural area where the speed limit had increased. I could easily get around both cars because a long straight stretch of road was visible across the small valley; there was no oncoming traffic. I pulled into the passing lane knowing, if I did not pass them now, I would be following behind for several miles.

Zip! Just like that the car was facing west, the wrong direction, in the passing lane then facing east, then west again in the ditch on the opposite side of the road.

"Is everyone okay? Tell me, each of you."

"Okay. Okay. Okay. Okay." Confident voices moved through the dark.

Taking inventory of myself, I told the kids I was also okay. Thankfully there had been no obstacles as we circled about on the slippery road.

Bobby Klingenmeyer, a young man from North Freedom, witnessed the Plymouth turn around and fly into the ditch. He shuffled across the ice and asked through the window if anyone was hurt before sliding into the driver's seat and limping our car to the shoulder and back onto the road toward home.

Melted snow had turned to black ice when the sun went down. The cars I passed had pulled over to check if there were injuries. I was sure those folks knew who I was. A lavender and white Plymouth is not easily disguised, not even in the dark of night.

Thinking about our memorable Plymouth reminds me of the gas wars in North Freedom. Those between Vic Kaldenberg and Obert Ulrich were pretty common. Gas could drop to unrealistic prices like eleven, ten, even nine cents a gallon. One of my older classmates filled all the five-gallon cans he could find and hauled them home to save for later.

Wayne Lankey delivered gas to our tank on the farm. We used gas for the truck and our tractors including the big red 2236 McCormick Deering with the crank start. That big tractor had the power-driven wheel used to run the threshing machine, silo filler and corn shredder. It could be switched to use kerosene, but we always used gasoline.

North Freedom had a car dealership. Dad bought his 1955 Chevy pickup truck uptown from Rist's Garage. He bought a new 1958 Chevy Bel Air in Reedsburg; the first time Dad ever paid over 3,000 dollars for a car. I loved that car. It was a beautiful light turquoise and white. However, the Chevy turned out to be a dud. Not long after Dad bought it, the transmission literally fell out onto State Highway 136 just west of the Ritz corners in Baraboo. The cost of the repair was covered by Chevy, but Dad and Mom agreed; it was never a great car. The lavender and white Plymouth that replaced the Chevy had a novel push button transmission, and the push buttons for changing gears were on the dashboard.

L to R: George and Faith Vertein's home, the former Seeley home; Myrtle and Ben Pawlisch's ranch house; Roy and Julia Ellas's home, their little woods beyond, 1963.

Neighbors

49

Elsie and Dan

Elsie and Dan Worth and Elsie's father, Charlie Lange, lived next door to us on the east end of Walnut Street. Elsie and Dan were in their fifties when I started grade school; Charlie was in his eighties. Their house was between ours and the railroad tracks. Elsie and Dan did not have children and loved my brothers and me; at least they paid us a lot of attention. We were allowed to visit them if we asked; Mom instructed us to behave and not get into their things. Elsie was short and wide and, like other ladies on the east end of Walnut Street, always wore dresses. She had little feet and walked by slightly swinging her round body from side to side. Elsie crocheted, packed Dan's lunch, put drops in Charlie's eyes and played Canasta. They ate fried potatoes, pickled herring and cottage cheese for supper on Friday night just like we did.

    I often accompanied Elsie on her walk to the post office uptown to collect our daily mail; she did not drive. We waved to neighbors from the sidewalk, but there were no extended conversations. We never ventured into homes, with one exception. Elsie lingered longer at Nellie Hackett's tiny place, the second house west of Depot Street.

North Freedom

My memories of Nellie were of a short, wrinkled woman of great age. When Nellie could no longer venture outside, Elsie and I entered the small room where Nellie sat on her worn sofa bed in a soft lump. She appeared delighted with these brief visits. Nellie's husband, Joseph, had died years before I was born. In *The Old Hackett's Homestead, Where North Freedom, Wisconsin Began*, my brother Allen writes, "Joseph was the son of Frank Hackett, a highly respected leader in the village ... Frank was the son of Samuel and Dency Hackett, the first settlers in what is now the Village of North Freedom." I had no idea of Nellie's background those days when I visited with her.

Elsie had two sisters. Polly was a teacher in Wisconsin Dells; Viola lived in Boynton Beach, Florida. Polly stood tall next to Elsie's short stature and was friendly like Elsie, but in more refined way. She gave used books to us. Viola looked like Elsie and had a jolly, contagious laugh like her sister's. However, Viola had a noticeable southern accent. She visited occasionally and brought tee shirts for my brothers and me with pictures on the front of sandy beaches, sailboats and palm trees. People from the village eyed the pictures when I wore the Florida tee shirts to the post office. Had this young lady visited Florida?

Elsie watched me crochet, corrected my errors and sometimes incorrectly corrected them. Mom sorted Elsie's mistakes. I ate only a couple of meals at Elsie's. I did not think her cooking was as good as Mom's, so I shied away from invitations to meals. Mom said Elsie did not use enough butter and onions or salt and pepper.

Elsie excelled at rosettes, those crisp deep-fried flowers dipped in sugar. Mom eventually mastered the art of these special cookies, but it required several attempts. This was not a bad thing because my brothers and I got to eat the rosettes that did not pass inspection. Elsie and Charlie taught me to play Canasta.

Dan worked in the stone quarry at LaRue. I never saw him at the quarry, but I knew the work he did was hard labor because of his sinewy muscled hands and arms. Mom sometimes made meat dinners for Elsie, Dan and Charlie. She said Elsie did not feed Dan enough meat, but that was because they did not have a farm. Often Mom and Dad had Dan help on the farm so they could serve him a good meal since hired men always ate at our house. Mom did not care if Elsie and Charlie ate at home alone those days. Elsie told Mom she packed mashed potato and oatmeal sandwiches in Dan's lunchbox. Elsie and Charlie ate their big meal at noon while Dan was at work. They all ate a smaller lunch together at suppertime.

Once every year, Elsie and Dan made homemade ice cream. They had a double metal canister machine with a crank. Using our cream, Elsie poured a rich mixture flavored with vanilla from the Watkins man into the inside container. Dan packed ice around it. Then his strong arms and shoulders turned the crank until his strained face showed the effort required to create this deliciousness. The ice cream was a grand treat. We ate it plain; sometimes strawberries were spooned over it. Elsie and Dan also made sherbet using newly fallen snow and pineapple. It was my favorite.

Walnut Street, 1944, looking west from the driveway where the Schroeder family lived beginning in 1948. The house on the upper farm is to the left. The steps and porch by the front door looked like this throughout the 1950s. Elsie and Dan Worth's home is to the right.

50

The South Side of East Walnut Street

An older couple, Dan and Mary Seeley, were our neighbors in the early 1950s. They lived in the lower level of the half-painted house on the south side of Walnut Street. Their home sat across the half mile road from the upper farm. The bottom half of the house was grayish white because years earlier Dan, a leader in the early days in the village, painted it as high as he could reach with a stepladder. The top half was never painted, so it was a sad dark weathered wood gray. Myrtle and Ben Pawlisch lived upstairs in the Seeley house in my earliest memory. They had lived on the other side of the Seeleys, but their house burned. Seeley's upstairs was their temporary residence while they built a new house in the same spot as the house they lost.

    Ben Pawlisch was a rural mail carrier working out of the North Freedom post office. Myrtle was a short round lady with red hair. She sang with a wobbly voice; it had a lot of vibrato. I sometimes heard her singing inside her home. Her voice was memorable, especially when amplified at the annual Memorial Day celebration at the cemetery. On that special day, we grade school children gathered by the post office and marched in the parade to the Oak Hill Cemetery north of town. "Lincoln's Gettysburg Address" was read, Lieutenant Colonel John McCrae's "In Flanders Fields" was recited, and Myrtle Pawlisch sang. A shiny microphone the size of a man's fist amplified her voice.

The most moving part of the ceremony was when local veterans took turns reading the names of each of their fellow veterans buried at the cemetery. An impressive presentation of arms followed with a thundering gun salute. As names were read, each of us children took a small wreath or flag and placed it on one of the white wooden crosses precisely placed in perfect formation in the open area by the war memorial. Boys placed the flags, and girls placed the wreaths. The wreaths were circles of stiff cardboard covered with green crepe paper with a bright red crepe paper flower bud attached. Green dye transferred from the wreaths to our sweaty hands, especially in warm humid weather. I was instructed not to touch my clothes until I washed away the green.

This celebration continues every year. I now recognize many more names as they are called; some are classmates. Several years ago, my husband and I joined the Freedom Singers for the musical part of the celebration following Myrtle Pawlisch's tradition.

Myrtle and Ben built a lovely ranch home next door to Seeley's, on the lot where their old house had burned. It was painted a light tan with white trim and was the first ranch style house I ever saw. Myrtle always purchased a white, heavily flocked Christmas tree from a florist for the holidays. It was usually the first one displayed on the east end of Walnut Street and sat in their corner picture window. A special white light or colored light wheel showcased the perfectly formed tree. When I saw Myrtle's flocked tree, I could hardly wait for Christmas.

The Pawlischs also had a shiny round gazing ball on a pedestal in their front yard and lots of colorful flowers. The outside of their place was beautiful every season. I never saw the inside of their home, but in my imagination its aesthetics matched the exterior.

Myrtle's maiden name was Deyhle. She was the daughter of George Deyhle, who along with Caesar Schenket, built a building uptown on the north side of Walnut Street. It was a meat market at the time. Myrtle must have liked her maiden name because she named one son Deyhle, and it is the middle name of her other son, Ronalddean.

When Myrtle and Ben moved into their new home, Jane Gunnison and her mom and dad moved in above the Seeley's. I never saw Jane's parents and was not allowed to play with her because she was a couple grades ahead of me. This made her a character of interest. Unfortunately, I never got to know her. Mom generally discouraged my brothers and me from playing with other children. Likely, the polio epidemic that was sweeping the country was a big influence for her to keep us away from other children. We had each other for playmates when we were young, and were expected to do farm work as soon as we were able. George and Faith Vertein bought the house from Mary Seeley sometime after Dan died. They had five children when they moved in but soon had seven. I babysat for the family.

Roy and Julia Ellas lived in the next house. It was actually a farm, but it did not look like a farm from the street. A little woods, the size of a lot, was west of their home. Behind their home and the little woods was a small barn and a workable field that stretched all the way to the river. Roy used a short part of the half mile road when doing his fieldwork. At the first corner of the road by the black walnut tree was an access gate that opened directly into his field.

The Ellas' were well into their sixties during the 1950s. Roy was a thin man and looked ancient. He had worked construction at Badger Ordnance Works in the early 1940s when the manufacturing facility was built for World War II. Roy's father, Stacy Pixley Ellas, operated a successful sawmill and lumberyard in the village years before.

"One of the Ellas girls is visiting." Mom usually knew what was happening on the east end of Walnut Street because she had a clear view out the front window from every room of our house all the way back to the kitchen. Lorraine Ellas was a nurse and occasionally came to our school or home when someone was sick. Mom could get notes from her to give to the school when we missed more than three days for illness. The Ellas' other daughter was Ethyl; she went by the name Butch. Butch's son, Craig, was my youngest brother Randy's classmate and helped on our farm after I was married.

On the other side of Ellas' little woods was the house on the big hill with the straight up and down driveway. Twin girls, Bonnie and Connie Kapelke, lived there. I went to grade school with them before they moved.

The last house before the empty lot on the corner of Walnut and Franklin Street was the Peterson's. Maynard was off to work most of the time, while Lenore stayed at home with the boys. She was always looking for them. Guy was a couple grades ahead of me. Carl was in Allen's class. Another of the Peterson's sons was killed in an accident before I could remember, so I understood why it was important to Lenore that she keep track of her boys. She had a loud voice. Allen said when Lenore called Carl to come home at suppertime, he could hear her on the lower farm on a clear day. That was not a total exaggeration, because Lenore came in loud and clear at the upper place no matter the direction of the wind.

The Petersons had a Christmas tree with a lot of lights in their window. The way the houses were built, and considering the people who lived in them, Pawlischs and Petersons were the only two homes with Christmas trees displayed so we could see them along the first block of the east end of Walnut Street.

The empty lot after Peterson's was the corner of Walnut and Franklin, the street where Grandma and Grandpa lived when they moved off the lower farm.

Irma Getschmann and Elsie (Lange) Worth attended a Schroeder family gathering at the North Freedom Rod and Gun Club, 1986.

51

The North Side of East Walnut Street

Harold and Sally Sorenson lived on the north side of Walnut Street, on the corner across from our house. They had girls: Dolly, Patsy, Ginger and a son, Ray. They also had a basketball hoop, the only one on the east end of Walnut Street.

The Sorenson girls babysat my brothers and me on those rare occasions our parents were gone, like when they attended the annual meeting of our dairy cooperative in Reedsburg. Another time the Sorenson girls babysat us was a special evening Mom and Dad joined a group to shivaree newlyweds, Phyllis and Herb Klein. The Kleins had just moved into their home out on Country Road PF, a few miles north of our farm. Mom and Dad later laughed about friends and neighbors banging on pots and pans as they continuously paraded around the Klein's home in the dark. Some created unique percussion gadgets for an even louder noise; others just whooped and hollered. The Kleins eventually came outside to join the celebration knowing it was the only way to stop the noise.

There was a lot of activity around the Sorenson place, like music and shooting hoops. Guys showed up in Baraboo

Thunderbird letter jackets, and high school kids came and went, sometimes by the carload. My fascination zeroed in on crinolines worn under full skirts in a multitude of colors, or long, narrow skirts, all at a length below the knee. The girls wore scarves in colors coordinating with their skirts, bobby socks and saddle shoes.

There was an empty lot between Sorensons and the next house where Irma Getschmann lived with her mother, Tilly, who did not venture outside. I was 10 years old when Tilly died at age 90. Irma had been a schoolteacher. She never married so there were no children. I loved her home because she had a lot of books. She occasionally gave some of them to our family.

Irma also gave an old mantle clock to my brothers. They hauled the clock around in the coaster wagon. They tried to fix it because it did not work, which is why Irma gave it to them in the first place. After the boys took it apart, they could not put it back together. However, they continued to haul the pieces around in the coaster wagon until Mom collected and stored the whole of it. Years later, that bucket of clock pieces was given to my husband, the skate boy. He crafted it back to chiming, keeping perfect time, and polished it to its original luster. It continues to grace a spot of honor high on top of our kitchen cupboards.

Irma and Elsie were friends, and friends of ours. From spring to fall they shared their screened porches with each other and with us. Mom let us kids go to their porches or homes one kid at a time; we were too rowdy as a group. Elsie dried black walnuts on each end of their porch in the fall. We were not to go near the walnuts; we had to stay in the middle of the porch.

We mostly talked to Elsie and Irma during our visits. They gave us their undivided attention, which was an enriching experience and different from being at home. I remember they laughed a lot. Elsie's laugh was a rolling jolly sound. Irma's was a high-pitched tee-hee-hee. Heaven only knows what I told them! We had a front porch, but it was not screened. We never once sat there because at home we either worked or played.

A large three-story home was directly west of Irma's. There was little activity around the place. The couple living there, Gordon and Yvonne Gaustad, kept to themselves. Mom, Elsie and Irma asked each other about them, but no one had answers to the questions.

Word in the neighborhood was that they were alcoholics—and—they were on the Black List of the county. My brothers and I had no idea what the Black List was—but it could not be good.

Yvonne was tall and sturdy. Her olive complexion was complimented with rows of dark soft curls at the top of her head, but the sides of her hair were clipped short to her scalp like a man's. She was the rare exception of a lady living on Walnut Street because she usually dressed in a dark brownish-green single piece work uniform, although she did not work at a job away from their home. I do not remember what Gordon looked like. He was seldom outside. The couple lived in the house several years before they abruptly moved away from North Freedom.

Gordon and Yvonne had a daughter, Beverly, who was disabled. My brothers and I saw Beverly sitting on a swinging bench or glider on their front porch in nice weather. We waved to her but never spoke. I felt sorry for Beverly because I did not think she had any friends. Later

North Freedom

I was uncomfortable knowing I saw her, but never talked to her. My brother David and his wife rented the house in the late 1960s. It was a lovely home.

Ricky, Bobby, Jerry and Duane Helms lived in the next house. Their parents were Gerald and Gusty, short for Augusta; they had an older sister, Carol, who no longer lived at home. Ricky was my bother David's age. The other boys were older than me. Bobby had girlfriends and drove cars. Jerry was a loner and rode the rails after he left home, which resulted in his untimely death.

Years later, I heard Jerry had become friends with his neighbors, Gordon and Yvonne Gaustad, and was on his way to join them when the accident happened. Duane married Donna Ramsey, a girl from Baraboo. Donna rode to work with me at Badger Army Ammunition Plant after I was married.

An older lady lived next to the Helms family. Her name, Marvel, fascinated me. Marvel and Tom Leece raised their family in that house before I can remember. One adult son occasionally visited Marvel after Tom died. Another son, Bill, married Evie; they lived kitty-corner across from his parents on the southwest corner of Franklin and Walnut Street.

Evie had a small beauty shop in their home. She cut my hair. A few times Mom paid the extra for Evie to curl my hair with rollers. On those occasions I sat under her hair dryer while hot air blew on my head until my ears turned bright red. She made my hair look beautiful, smooth, not frizzy. I wished it would stay that way forever. (My brothers sat on the white metal stool in the kitchen of our farmhouse when Dad cut their hair with the hand clipper, later the electric clipper.) Donald, known as Pete, another of Marvel and Tom's sons, married Marian, my piano teacher's daughter. Marian's younger brother, Rollie, was my classmate for twelve years.

Clarence and Delores Vondran built a new white ranch home on the lot past Leece's while I was still in grade school. It was built in front of Phil and Alice Zimmerly's small house that sat back closer to the railroad tracks. We used the narrow sidewalk branching off the main walk to get to Phil and Alice's front door for our occasional visits. Phil was the first maintenance man for the village and got the village snowplow stuck in the lower corner of our half mile road during the Blizzard of 1959.

Clarence and Delores were Catholic, which was unusual; everyone else on the east end of Walnut Street went to one of the churches in town, or not at all. The Vondrans had to drive to Baraboo for church. Clarence was a carpenter and Delores stayed home with their three daughters. I babysat the girls when I was in high school.

I could name folks living in each house along Walnut Street all the way uptown as well as in most houses throughout the village. However, I knew those at the east end of Walnut Street best.

Harold and Edith (Easy) Beckman, circa 1940s. Harold was Pearl Schroeder's cousin. Harold's father, Rudy, was Grandma Hilda (Beckman) Kaun's half-brother.

Visits

52

Harold and Easy

We took day trips, not long vacations, because our cows needed to be milked twice each day. Once a year we visited Mom's cousin who lived by Truax Field on the northeast side of Madison. After chores one morning, Mom and Dad loaded my brothers and me into the back seat of our 1941 Chevy coupe and headed towards the bluffs.

The highway went around an outcropping of granite that stood close to the road a couple miles south of Baraboo. Mom and Dad explained the huge rock was unique because the glaciers had not ground it to gravel, and University of Wisconsin geology students studied it. Ski-Hi Apple Orchard was visible on the hill toward Devils Lake just before the road changed from two lanes to a four-lane highway going over the bluff to the prairie.

The powder plant, Badger Ordnance Works, lay on the prairie on the other side of the bluff. The facility closed after World War II, but reopened to manufacture gunpowder for the Korean Conflict in the early 1950s and was now in full operation.

As a five-year-old, I curiously studied the plant because sometimes we heard faraway booms in North Freedom.

North Freedom

Mom and Dad told us they came from the powder plant. I listened for explosions as we passed by. I heard none.

The plant was big. The parking lot was a field of hundreds of cars. I learned this section of road was the first four-lane highway in Wisconsin, built to accommodate the massive number of vehicles needed to construct the plant and produce gunpowder for World War II after Japan attacked Pearl Harbor on December 7, 1941.

The powder plant looked like a prison. I heard this comparison as a child, and although I never saw a prison, I knew they were not nice. There was barbed wire at the top of the chain link fence surrounding the powder plant. Small wooden lookouts were constructed above the fence and were incrementally spaced along the west side of the plant adjacent to the highway. Mom and Dad explained security guards sat in the lookouts. My brothers and I slunk low in the backseat with the uncomfortable feeling of someone spying into our car.

A lot of folks from North Freedom worked there. Mom said a man from North Freedom was killed at the plant during World War II when a nitroglycerin building exploded. She and almost everyone in North Freedom heard the BOOM. Later, the man's youngest son, Edwin, was my classmate at the North Freedom grade school. The place was sobering, and I was glad when we were once again driving along fields of clover and oats.

My brothers and I sat in the backseat with empty cottage cheese containers on our laps because we were prone to getting carsick. As we rode to Madison, Mom lectured us on the "dos and don'ts" of our visit and how we were to mind her and Dad—immediately. Harold and Easy did not have children, and I suspect Mom did not want us to be a reason to discourage them from starting a family.

Mom's cousin, Harold Beckman, was married to Easy. Her real name was Edith, but everyone called her Easy because that was what Harold called her. She did not seem to mind. She was a tall, slender brunette resembling Lauren Bacall, especially when she wore her fashionable suit jackets with the wide padded shoulders. She appeared sophisticated and was an accomplished pianist. She had taught music in Joliet, Illinois, while Harold was in service overseas before they were married. I wanted to be like Easy when I grew up.

Harold was laidback and full of jokes. He had a HAM radio in the basement of their home along with a great pinball machine and all sorts of mechanical and electronic games and gadgets.

Harold and his brother, Leo, as well as several cousins, served in the military during World War II. Cousin Norman died in the Battle of Normandy; his body was never found. Mom and Dad first met at Norman's memorial service in Reedsburg. Dad traveled to the service from Caledonia, Minnesota. His mother, Wilhelmine, was Norman's aunt, a sister to Norman's father. Norman's mother, Alma, was a half-sister to Grandma Hilda and Mom's aunt. Mom and Dad were each attending their respective cousin's memorial service.

Years later I read in Harold's obituary he was "in the Pacific War (1942-1946) and Master Sergeant 126th Radio Intelligence. He was one of the first operators to make radio contact to Tokyo on VJ Day from Allied Supreme Command."

Once we arrived at their home, we walked quietly into Harold and Easy's living room and sat on the couch waiting for the cue allowing us to go to the basement. When it was time, we scrambled down the stairs before there might be some reason to stop us. Harold handed over stacks of coins to play pinball; it was my favorite. The men played pool while the HAM radio chattered in the background.

All too soon it was lunchtime. We did not want to leave the basement, but Easy always served kid food like hotdogs and potato chips. We ate farm food at home so Easy's meals were a huge treat.

We expected to go directly to the basement when we finished eating that day; however, Mom told us to wait. "Easy is going to play the piano for us." I think Mom told Easy she wanted me to start lessons. Easy's piano was in a tiny alcove off the living room. My brothers and I were lined in a row on the couch with a stern look from Mom. Be good! Sit still! Listen!

Easy played her own involved special arrangement of "Deep Purple". There were many runs where her long slender fingers moved deftly from one end of the keyboard to the other with soft pianissimos and exploding crescendos.

At last it was over.

Harold's wide smile showed appreciation as he surveyed our lineup on the couch. "What did you think of that?" His eyebrows raised like he expected an answer.

I smiled broadly not sure what to say.

After an awkward silence David piped up seriously, "If I pounded on the piano like that Mama would spank me."

Mom's face drained of color.

Thankfully, Easy started to laugh. "Well. No one has ever said that before." David had no idea he had said anything wrong. He was being honest. Thankfully, we were hustled back to the basement.

53

Maple Syrup

Ruth (Tewes) and Herb Holzman and their boys, Artie and Jimmy, had a farm in the bluffs beyond LaRue close to the Maple Hill Apple Orchard. Ruth and Mom were cousins. A small hillside of sugar maple trees was on their property. Herb tapped these trees with metal spigots when frosty winter temperatures turned to spring thaw.

When our family arrived to help the Holzman's with the seasonal task of making maple syrup, sap was already dripping into metal buckets that were hung within our reach on the taps. Our visits with the Holzman family were coordinated during this first warm weather when buckets filled fast and heating the sap began.

My brothers and I heard dripping as we approached the small woods. We, along with Artie and Jimmy, hauled half-full buckets of raw maple sap down the side hill back to the farm to the long flat evaporation pans that sat in a bed of glowing coals. Adults emptied our buckets into these heating pans, and we hurried them back to the trees to catch more sap. Each tree produced about ten gallons. The adults told us not to let the buckets get full. We were ages 6 to 11 at the time and could not manage full buckets. Plus, it was important that no sap be spilled. We had to scurry to keep up with the trees at the height of production.

Herb tended the fire under the evaporation pans so it provided a low consistent temperature that continually simmered the sap without burning it. As moisture evaporated from the pans, the temperature of the residual sap would rise and more sap had to be added or the concentrated mixture would burn. Once this process started it did not stop, even if it meant staying up continuously for several days and nights. It takes about forty gallons of sap to make one gallon of syrup. Our family traveled to and from the Holzman home over the course of several days during this time. Mom took soup, chili and ham for sandwiches, along with many of her tasty bars and cookies. We picked handfuls of early violets and johnny jump ups in the woods for Mom and Ruth.

Sap produces a sugar sand known as niter as it is concentrated. Herb and Ruth filtered the concentrated sap to remove niter and any other debris that might have gotten into the syrup like twigs, leaves, bugs or ash from the fire. The final purification process was to bring the syrup into the house, boil it on the wood stove and drop egg whites into it. Any debris or impurities would cling to the egg whites and float to the top to be scooped out and thrown away, leaving behind pure maple syrup.

Our families got together again at our house when we received a portion of syrup for our help. Mom served a light meal at this event. The adults played card games: euchre, 500 or sheepshead, while my brothers and I played with Artie and Jimmy outside or in our playroom in the basement.

54
George and Emma Davies

George and Emma Davies lived in North Freedom, across from Grandma and Grandpa's house on Franklin Street. George Davies had been County Superintendent of Schools for Sauk County. He had also been principal of the North Freedom Elementary School in the early 1900s.

The following details were found in the *Good Old Golden Rule Days* book, where additional information about the school is documented along with articles about the other schools in the area. The "County Superintendent's Annual Report" of 1898 lists the North Freedom School as brick with three rooms and an 1880 building date. There were three teachers, primary, intermediate and upper with George W. Davies as principal and third teacher. A two-year high school started in 1902 and was conducted in an annex across the street from the elementary school. Mr. Davies remained in charge of the high school until 1906 when he became County Superintendent of Schools."

Mr. and Mrs. George, as we called them, had a rock garden of flowers and a variety of plants in an adjacent lot north of their home. Grandpa Louie had a great deal of respect for George Davies because of Davies' leadership in the village, his work at the school, and his extensive knowledge of plants. However, Grandpa considered the large rock garden a waste of time, energy and land. I thought it was beautiful. Grandma agreed with me, but neither of us was about to contradict Grandpa. Mrs. George shared her plants with Grandma: hen and chicks, a succulent plant with stiff, pointed leaves; frog's tongue, a taller plant with flat leaves; and a variety of cactus plants. These plants grew in the sandy soil along the walk on the south side of Grandma and Grandpa's house between a mound of iris and a string of gladiolus.

Grandma had other plants from Mrs. George in her sunroom, the small southeast sitting room off the kitchen of their home. I watered these plants using the little yellow watering can with the long narrow spout on those special days I spent with Grandma. I also added water to the small ceramic bowls that sat on the steam radiators of their home; this added humidity to the air especially during cold dry Wisconsin winters. The water also created a crusty residue of minerals on the bowls because of the hard water of our area. These heavy grey bowls decorated with Native American designs were known as Sleepy Eye stoneware. They came packed in 50-pound bags of flour from a milling company in Sleepy Eye, Minnesota. One of the bowls, a fond memory, graces the upper cabinets of our kitchen today, next to Irma Getschmann's clock.

Mrs. George made orange blossom treats, small biscuits soaked in orange sauce with zest. They were my favorite. A couple of times every year, when I was visiting Grandma alone, Mrs. George invited us into their home. It was like a fairyland of beautiful old dishes, stately furniture, fresh flowers, a piano, a formally set table and lots of books; my eyes could hardly take in all the loveliness. Their granddaughter,

Alice, was about my age, but she did not live close by and was not able to visit her grandparents often. I think they enjoyed my visits because they missed their granddaughter.

I delivered the Davies' personal mail for several years starting when I was ten years old. Unlike our mail, I had to ask the postmaster, Bob Myers, for theirs since I did not have the combination for their box. I opened their enclosed front porch door and laid the mail on an ottoman to the right. Mom and Grandma said not to step into the porch. At the end of each week there was an envelope with my name on it sitting on the ottoman. It held two dollars. When I started working as a live-in nanny in Wisconsin Dells at age fifteen, Allen took over the mail delivery job.

Each summer our family spent a couple of days at the Davies' cottage on Mirror Lake, about 10 miles northeast of the farm. The cottage had to be set up the day before our arrival. Dad hauled water in 10-gallon milk cans. Wooden shutters on the screened windows were eased open just enough to circulate air, but minimize humidity seeping into the rooms during the night. Inventory was taken of dishes, silverware, cookware, fishing poles, bedding, pillows and gas for the 5-horse Martin motor on our boat. There were more of us than the Davies' clan, so we had to supplement extra supplies.

Mom prepared food at home and packed it in our small metal cooler because there was no refrigerator at the cottage. She depended on us to catch and clean fish for several meals. Our catch was dipped in flour and pan-fried in butter in a cast iron pan on the small gas stove.

One treat was when Dad took us out on the lake in our small boat to fish. At the cottage, we waded through lily pads by the heavy chunk of a split log that served as the dock.

None of us knew how to swim at that time. When the boat sat empty at the dock, we grabbed our cane poles, bobbers and worms and clambered into it for some serious fishing. We could toss our bait further from shore hoping to pull in more fish. We caught perch, pumpkin seeds and bluegills that we scaled and cleaned on a propped board between the small garage and the outhouse behind the cottage.

A special part of our visits was sleeping in the cottage since I hardly ever stayed overnight anywhere away from home. I slept in an old metal bed in a small bedroom or on the daybed on the screened porch. The bedding was clean, but a musty smell permeated the air that I did not notice until I lay quietly in the still of the evening, waiting for sleep.

There was a small library of children's books at the cottage, and a container of pick-up sticks and a box of dominoes. Mom always brought a deck of playing cards.

When we were not in the water or fishing, we played on the double bench glider sitting on the empty adjacent lot. The glider belonged to the Farber's next door, but we were allowed to use it if we did not swing too high.

Grandma and Grandpa stopped by during the day to fish and share a meal, but did not stay because there were limited sleeping accommodations. On a few special days I went alone with Grandma and Grandpa to the cottage. It was unusual to not have my brothers near me during those visits, and while it was a treat to have time by myself, after a while it could get boring.

The Davies' offered their cottage at other times, too. However, our family never considered abusing their kindness by overstaying our welcome.

55

Herman and Idella

When I was in early grade school, I spent a week each summer with Herman and Idella Schroeder on their farm in Caledonia, Minnesota. They were my aunt and uncle, but, with permission, I called them by their given names. During the upper grades my stay extended to two weeks. Herman and Idella did not have children; their first child died shortly after birth, and a second child was still-born. They were fun to be around because they acted and reacted like children themselves during my stay.

Herman was Dad's older brother, and Idella had been Dad's teacher at the Winnebago School, a one room building for all eight grades, about two miles across adjacent open fields from the Schroeder family farm. Dad carried love letters between his older brother and his teacher when he attended grade school.

I was eight years old on my first visit. At that time Herman and Idella's house did not have indoor plumbing. Water had to be pumped by hand in the tiny pantry off the kitchen where there was a galvanized dry sink and open shelves holding pots and pans, spices and all the gadgets needed to prepare meals and for baking. There were no cupboards with closing doors.

North Freedom

The kitchen seemed small because of the huge heavy metal cook stove on the south wall that was fired up the first thing every morning no matter how hot it was outside. Idella made lefse on the bare range top and baked Sprutbackels, Norwegian butter cookies, in the oven. A small three burner gas range was installed later. The little stove was used only for emergencies, a quick meal if the fire was low in the big stove or for extra cooking space when needed. The floor, covered with linoleum, slanted noticeably to the south. Their kitchen was a converted summer kitchen, like the summer kitchen in the old house on our lower farm. Houses had been built that way so the heat of the wood stove would not unduly overheat other rooms. There was a chrome-style kitchen set with chair seats covered in light gray vinyl that had a marble pattern typical of the 1950s. The pattern of the vinyl matched the tabletop.

The most interesting thing in the kitchen was the telephone. We did not have a telephone at home until I was twelve years old. Theirs was a big wooden box hanging on the wall with a metal horn shaped mouthpiece for speaking, a candlestick receiver for listening and a crank for making calls.

The mouthpiece moved up and down to accommodate people of various heights. The receiver hung on a U hook on the left side of the telephone. The U hook moved up when the phone was "off the hook" and was held down by the receiver when the phone was not in use. The crank on the right side of the wooden box was used to get in touch with the operator or to call a neighbor on the party line. One long crank yielded one long ring of the phone and was the ring that connected the caller to the operator. Only operators at central telephone stations could place calls beyond the neighborhood party line.

One could call other people on their party line directly without going through the operator. That was done by using different combinations of long and short turns of the crank. These cranks resulted in the same combinations of long and short rings on all the phones in the various homes connected to the party line. Each household had to count the long and short rings to determine if a phone call was meant for them.

Herman and Idella were on a nine-party line; nine different families shared one telephone line. Only one party, family, could be making a call at any specific time. It was not unusual to pick up the receiver and hear folks talking. Sometimes one family, or person, monopolized the line.

When Idella needed to make a call and another person was talking, she first softly replaced the receiver on the hook. After what Idella felt was a reasonable period of time to complete a conversation, she butted in and said, "We need to make a call." She then waited for the person to hang up the phone while she continued to listen to their conversation. Sometimes Idella let me check to see if the line was busy. I could listen if a conversation was in progress but not for long; that was rude.

Idella called one neighbor, who was on their party line, to schedule time for me to visit their daughter, Judy. Judy's ring was two shorts and three longs. Idella gave the crank two quick grinding half turns, then three long grinding double turns to call Judy's house. To call Mom and Dad it was necessary for Idella to talk to the operator.

Herman and Idella's house had a combination dining and living room. It was a dining room in the middle because a heavy oak table and matching chairs sat there. It was a living room around the edges. A deep red vinyl sofa covered with an afghan sat against the north wall; Herman's cushioned chair was on the south.

A large oak desk was in the northeast corner of the room. Herman was active in agricultural politics in Minneapolis and Saint Paul, and the desk was usually covered with papers Herman sifted through when he was not outside or napping in his chair. There was a metal-sheathed oil stove in the middle of the west wall, between the door to Herman and Idella's bedroom and the door to the steep stairs leading to the second floor.

Like our family, Herman and Idella did not have television. They played card games and fabricated entertainment for me by using their imaginations. I begged them to start what they called "The Pipe Stories." These were stories we made up as we told them. Herman and Idella told me there was a Pipe family, a mom and dad and a boy and girl. Herman started the story saying the Pipes did this or that. In short order he became very animated and continued with something like, "Mr. Pipe was walking alone in the dark forest when he heard something rustle the leaves behind him, so he hid behind a spruce tree and did not make a sound. After waiting a long time, he peeked around the tree and saw a large, hairy"—"Carolyn." He would say my name abruptly and stop talking midsentence. I had to continue the story. "Wolf," I would say and start to giggle as I thought of an even greater event. My story was continued until I stopped and said—"Idella."

One time Idella said, "Santa Claus." This surprised me because I had expected her to say something scary. We all had a good laugh as she continued the story. Back in North Freedom, I would conjure new Pipe family stories to tell on my next visit. I imitated Herman's animation because I knew it would add to my story and to their entertainment.

There were two bedrooms, Herman and Idella's off the dining room and the small one I used at the top of the steep narrow stairs. Another room upstairs could have been a bedroom, but was used for storage. The house had no basement.

There was no bathroom. An outhouse sat outside, behind the single car garage. A white pot at the end of my bed was to be used if I had to go to the bathroom during the night. I never used it because I was not keen about having to empty the thing. I was in the upper grades of elementary school when Herman and Idella got indoor plumbing. This provided the luxury of water for the kitchen and fabricating a small bathroom with a basin, toilet and bathtub off the dining room.

Herman owned a threshing machine that he shared with four neighboring farm families. When the first fields of grain ripened within this collective, Herman hauled his machine to that farm. All of the families in this community group gathered to bring in that crop before the machine was hauled to the next farm. This benefited all the farmers because the others did not have to invest in, maintain or store a threshing machine, and Herman had a full crew of men and boys to harvest his crop.

Starting when I was ten years, old my visits were arranged during threshing activities. I was expected to help prepare and clean up after the mammoth meals needed to feed the threshing crew. Grain ripens in August, and threshing lasted several days at Herman and Idella's farm. The big wood burning stove in the small kitchen was stoked day and night for a fire that kept an even temperature for roasting chickens, beef and pork, and for baking bread, cookies and pies, Idella's specialties. The stifling weather made no difference; the fire was maintained for preparing meals.

I met kids on the crew, mostly boys, and recognized them when I returned the following years. I remembered the most interesting boys from year to year, but there was little time to spend together because threshing required continuous work. The harvest stopped abruptly a few days before I returned to North Freedom. Communication between the boys and me was virtually impossible once I returned home. Undoubtedly Mom and Dad preferred that.

56

My Bicycle

I wanted a bicycle. I learned to ride at Aunt Edna and Uncle Rudolph's farm in Caledonia, Minnesota. The trip was a big treat for our family and did not happen often because our leaving meant Grandpa Louie had to do chores and milk cows without Dad's help. I was six years old when we visited that day, and I was determined I would learn to ride a bicycle before we returned home. I knew from previous visits they had a girl's bike. It was their daughter Eleanor's, who was now 20 years old. Most of our cousins were considerably older than my brothers and me. This was because Dad was the second youngest of the eleven Schroeder boys, and he did not get married until he was 34 years old. There were no cousins on Mom's side of the family because Mom was an only child. Eleanor's bicycle was a rare opportunity for me to learn to ride.

It was a three-hour drive from North Freedom through the Wildcat Mountains to La Crosse and the 20 miles on to Caledonia. We took a county road southeast out of Caledonia to the long gravel driveway curving between rolling fields to Rudolph and Edna's farm. The barn and other buildings sat on the top of a hill at the end of the drive.

While Mom and Dad stretched their arms and legs, my brothers and I anxiously scrambled out of the backseat.

Several of my aunts and uncles were already coming down the narrow walk, past the small grove of pine trees to the gate dividing the parking area and farm buildings from the long gentle slope of lawn leading up to the farmhouse. This was where my Dad and his ten brothers grew up. It was where Mom and Dad were living when I was born.

I was impatient for family greetings to end and finally interjected, "Could I use your bicycle please?" Eager to accommodate their young guests, my cousins collected the bike and rolled it across the grass to the gate. I grabbed the handlebars with authority and pushed the heavy thing a short distance up the sloping lawn toward the house. Having attempted to master this same bicycle on an earlier visit, I thought it would be easier to maintain my balance if I started maneuvering slowly over a short distance. Injuries would be minimal if I fell, and I could learn how to stop the thing.

I hopped on and had not gone three feet before I tipped over; the adults headed toward the house, probably wanting to avoid an impending disaster. I struggled to right the bike and tried again. I tipped over again, then pushed the bike back to my starting point. Eventually, I managed to stay upright all the way to the gate. Elated, I pushed the bike farther up the slope toward the house and continued this trial and error riding for several hours.

After many minor crashes, I could do it! I repeatedly pushed the heavy bike up the entire slope to the farmhouse and, with my feet on the pedals, coasted to the fence. One time I smiled at Dad from my perch on the wide seat and pushed on the pedals to increase speed. This promptly caused me to lose my footing. My knee and hand hit the ground. Little dots of blood oozed through green grass stains embedded in my skin. Dad checked me over and explained how to use the pedals to control speed. I let my knee and hand burn, and tried again until I got the hang of coordinating speed and braking.

I never hit the fence or the gate. I could pedal on flatland, but when I tried riding up the slope, the heavy bike would not cooperate. When I stood on the pedals and strained to move the wide tires uphill, I always lost my balance.

The afternoon waned. Uncle Rudolph sent his boys, Rueben and John, to start chores and to let the dog out to roundup cows from the pasture to the barn for milking. The dog had been in the barn all day and wanted to join the fun before going to work. He ran through the now open gate toward the people conversing on the walk along the slope. This happened at exactly the same time I was making a last pass down the hill on the bike. The dog's attention diverted; he probably had not seen the bike for some time. The dog ran toward me. I panicked. We ran into each other.

Scared and possibly hurt, the dog grabbed me around my left side. Ouch! He let go immediately, but there were tiny dent marks in my side from his teeth. "It was an accident. I didn't mean to run into him!" I cried but was not hurt, except for my pride. My aunt and uncle were more concerned about me than Mom and Dad; although the adults concurred, the bites did not warrant further attention. It was soon time for the long drive home. Exhausted, my brothers and I slept in the car.

The next evening Mom called to Dad as she was preparing bath water. I stood beside her ready to jump into the tub. "Look. What do you think?" I was a sorry sight. Black and blue bruises now showed head to toe from an afternoon of tipping over on the bicycle. Little red dogtooth dents stood out on my side.

"Aw. She'll be alright." Dad was not concerned and neither was I, but I was surprised at how beat up I looked.

Now that I had ridden the Minnesota bicycle, I wanted my own. I did not think that would ever happen—until we went to an auction out on County Road W later that year. There it was, a girl's bike. It was a beautiful bright blue with a black leather seat and shiny metal handlebars. The bike was heavy with wide fenders and tires. It was perfect.

I waited patiently for what seemed like all day before the bike was auctioned. Dad was toward the front of the crowd. I was standing off in a field by Mom. Dad told me he would bid on the bike but not to get my hopes up because it was such a nice bike. He figured other people would probably bid against him. I could not understand the auctioneer's lingo but knew the longer the bidding continued the higher the price would be.

As the auctioneer's voice droned on, my hopes dwindled. "Sold."

I could not see Dad. Where was he? Shortly, he appeared at the edge of the crowd and came strolling slowly across the cornfield toward me with his head down, without the bike. He glanced at my anxious face, stopped and slowly shook his head to one side. I was devastated—momentarily—before Dad smiled. "It's your bike, Susie. Go get it."

I jumped up and down, beyond excited. A lot of people must have been watching me because years later, even after I was married, I could be somewhere in North Freedom and someone I did not know would say, "Aren't you the little Schroeder girl that got that blue bike at the auction out on W?"

I was surprised how Dad did not want to let me know right off his bid bought the bicycle. I think he wanted to be close to me so he could share my excitement. We did not disappoint each other.

Top: L to R: Artie Holzman and Carolyn and David Schroeder collect pails of maple sap from Holzman's sugarbush. The children are standing in front of the long flat evaporation pans on the Holzman farm on Maple Hill. A 10-gallon milk can is sitting behind the pan on the right side of the picture. If the pans were full while sap was being collected, the extra sap was held in the 10-gallon can until the evaporation process caught up with sap collection. *Bottom*: L to R: David, Allen, and Carolyn fish from their family's boat at the makeshift wooden dock in front of George and Emma Davies's cottage at Mirror Lake in Lake Delton, Wisconsin, summer 1956.

Top: North Freedom Grade School (Photo compliments of the Sauk County Historical Society). *Bottom*: Carolyn Schroeder's Report Card from the 1953–1954 school year.

North Freedom Grade School

57
My Early Years

The North Freedom Grade School was uptown, three blocks west of our house and south on Oak Street, around the corner behind Gehrmann's grocery store. It was a two-story red brick building, one of the two biggest buildings in the village. *The Good Old Golden Rules Days* by the Rural Schools Research Committee, Sauk County Historical Society, Baraboo, Wisconsin, 1994, describes the school as follows:

> The ... elementary school was brick and was erected in 1902. In the 1920's an auditorium and gymnasium were added. At this time ... a charter for a four year high school was obtained. All 12 grades were conducted in the large brick building ... The high school was discontinued in 1945. High school students attended Baraboo High School and the district paid tuition. North Freedom joined the Baraboo School System in 1961 and continued to operate the grade school.

Mom graduated as an honor student from North Freedom High School in 1943 when this same building housed all grade and high school students. Classmates graduating with her were: Alvin Kowalke, Olive Kuhnau, Albert Pawlisch Jr., Leah Gaetzke, Robert Ulrich, Ruby Lyons Curtis, Norbert Albers, Ruth Shimniok, Clarence Vorndran, Maurice Hughes, John Burmester and Arloween Licht. Mom occasionally mentioned their names, but only in passing. I knew several of these people because they continued to live in the village or the surrounding area. The concept of Mom as a student did not register with me until I was an adult. I wish I had paid more attention and asked more questions about her days as a student.

The 1920 addition included classrooms to the south of the auditorium and gymnasium. One of these rooms was used as a science lab. Lower classrooms were converted to our lunchroom by the time my brothers and I attended the grade school. Refrigerators used to cool milk cartons were also in these rooms.

There were four classrooms with two grades in each. First through fourth grade were in the two classrooms on the first floor; fifth through eighth grade were on the second floor. This changed slightly during the mid-1950s because the number of children in each incoming grade increased significantly because of the baby boomers. Some grades were split during that time to accommodate the number of students and not overwhelm the teachers.

All rooms had hardwood floors with a glossy shine, at least at the beginning of the school year. An open staircase in the center of the building had a wide landing, dividing the stairs into two sections. At the top of the staircase, directly above the front entry, was the principal's office.

I started school as a first grader in 1953. There was no kindergarten. Miss Brimmer, my teacher, was not much taller than her students. Like the other women teachers at our school, she always wore dresses. Her black leather shoes were tied with fine black shoestrings and had a medium-high square heel. Miss Brimmer must have had her hands full when I started first grade because there were thirty-seven children in her classroom. We were the first of the baby boomers. The following year, I, along with some of my classmates, went to the third and fourth grade classroom to balance the student count.

I did not know what to expect when I received my first report card. I had no idea what it was. Mom seriously studied the report before she and Dad explained what it meant. They did not make a big deal out of my grades. Academic work was graded with A, B, C, or D with A being the highest or best grade; skills were graded with S for satisfactory and U for unsatisfactory. My card had marks of A, B, and S, although some were followed by a minus sign. Mom and Dad said they expected my next report card to be similar, and I was to continue keeping up with my classwork. My parents never showed disappointment in my grades, although not all of my report cards were as good as the first.

We started each day by standing with our faces turned to our classroom flag, hands over our hearts, and reciting the Pledge of Allegiance. My first-grade desk was a piece of finished wood with a long indentation to hold a pencil at the top, a hole for an inkwell, and had a cubbyhole underneath for paper, crayons, scissors and workbooks. The sides of the cubbyhole were made of iron filigree type scroll work. The upper grade desks had a wood-looking writing surface that raised up to open a metal compartment to store textbooks and school supplies. These desks had an attached seat that usually did not properly fit students at the beginning of the school year.

Augie, our first janitor, and later Mr. Crawford, made the rounds and adjusted the length and height from the seat to the writing surface to fit each student. Allen was in seventh grade when Mr. Crawford died. Each class went over to the

Methodist Church to view the body and pay respects. I was a freshman at Baraboo Junior High School by that time so did not participate.

Classes were structured so teachers could cover all subjects for two grades. Each classroom had a library in a corner or under the windows, consisting of several shelves of books. I depended on the school's library because the village library was one small room in the village hall with a minimum number of children's books. The village library had limited hours that were not a good fit with my farm chores. Our music lessons were broadcast on a big wooden console radio from a station out of Madison.

The Weekly Reader, a student newspaper, covered current events. I was in fourth grade when I read about the upcoming election. President Eisenhower was currently serving. Although Truman was President when I was born, Eisenhower had been president as long as I could remember. We talked about politics at home, but I did not know how Eisenhower came to be president. What would happen if that changed? I was stunned. I never forgot the insecurity I felt that day. I talked to Mom and Dad about the election article, wondering if it was true. They assured me elections were part of living in a democracy, and that it had happened many times. I later wrote a paper titled "Why I Like Living in a Democracy." It won first place in a contest while I was in grade school.

58

Telephone

When my grade school classmate, Terri Thomas, told me their family had a wooden crank telephone on the wall when she was a little kid, I thought about how lucky she was. I was twelve years old when we got our first telephone; it was a desk model. Terri was the oldest of five children and smart as a whip.

One day while her mother was taking care of one of the babies, Terri decided to make a call. She pulled a kitchen chair over to the wall phone and climbed up so she could reach the crank. She gave it a turn.

"I need to make a call," she told the operator. Grace Cole, "Gracie," manned the switchboard in a room above the North Freedom Bank uptown. She had taken over the switchboard in 1950 following Gladys Sullivan who had held the job for many years.

The little voice probably alarmed Gracie. "Can you tell me who you are?" she asked.

"I'm Terri Thomas."

"Hello, Terri." Gracie smiled. "Who is it you would like to call?"

"I'd like to call Santa Claus, please." Terri said her request likely made the poor woman laugh out loud.

Gracie was obviously a quick thinker because she recalled an older gentleman who lived close to the Thomas family.

"Well, Terri, I need to look around for Santa. You wait on the phone until I find him. Can you do that?"

"Okay."

Gracie rung up the older gentleman. "Could you help me? I have the little Thomas girl on the phone. Her family lives over by you. She wants to speak to Santa Claus. Do you think you could talk to her for a bit? Her name is Terri."

Terri said the older gentleman and Gracie were probably both enjoying her call by now.

"Sure, I could talk to Terri." He hesitated. "Uhm—what should I say?"

"Just ask her what she wants and let her talk," Gracie encouraged. She popped back into Terri's phone. "I have Santa Claus on the line. You can go ahead and talk to him."

Terri remembered she was having this great conversation with Santa Clause when she heard, "What are you doing?" Audrey, her mother, was standing at the kitchen door, stunned. "Who are you talking to?" Audrey had listened long enough to realize Terri was not pretending to talk to someone; there was a real person on the other end of the line.

"I'm talking to Santa Claus," Terri exclaimed proudly.

Terri laughed and said that was the end of her first telephone call.

One reason we got our telephone was because when we got rid of the bull, we needed to call for artificial insemination for our cows. We continued to use Elsie's telephone for a while after the bull was gone, but this got to be too much bother with the need to call so frequently. Also, the grade school principal, Harold Pickar, called the Verteins to take messages to Mom. Some were not pleasant. The Verteins were our neighbors across the half mile road at this time.

After one big snowstorm, Dad drove us to school earlier than usual. The school doors were still locked, because the doors did not open until the janitor rang the first bell. We had to be in our seats by the time he rang the second bell. Parents were discouraged from having their children arrive early for school in those days. Since we usually arrived about the time the first bell rang, we were surprised to see a good number of classmates already congregated outside the front door. Several were crying and complaining about waiting in the cold. Some banged on the door to be let in before first bell.

Harold Pickar and the teachers were upset that all these freezing and complaining children were begging to get into the school, so Mr. Pickar gave a detention to all the children who had arrived early. The goal was to deter early arrivals so he and the teachers would not need to put up with us again the next day and in the future. Mr. Pickar said, "It's wrong of parents to make children stand outside in the cold before the first bell."

My brothers and I worried because we each received a detention. We told Mom. Mom, in turn, wrote a pointed note to Mr. Pickar, explaining that Dad had to work around the storm on the farm and brought us to school when he had a chance. She also made it clear we were never late, and he ought to be happy we were early instead of late. In fact, she had never heard of a detention for children getting to school early.

Mr. Pickar was not happy when he read Mom's note, but removed our detentions. Since we did not have a telephone, Mr. Pickar called the Verteins. He told Faith Vertein to let Mom know what he thought of the note and to tell Mom she should have her children at school at the proper time. We got our own telephone after that fiasco.

Top: First and second grades of North Freedom school, 1953–1954. Carolyn is fifth from the left in the second row. *Bottom*: The number of children in classes in 1956 was much larger than in previous years. This was because of the baby boom following World War II. Some grades had to be split between teachers and classrooms. Carolyn is first on the left in the third row.

59

Lunch and Recess

We had milk breaks in the mid-morning. Until third grade, only white whole milk was served, first out of glass bottles, later in individual waxed cartons. At home, we drank raw milk from our cows, so pasteurized milk tasted strange to me. Mom let cream rise to the top of raw milk at home. She poured off the cream and used it for cooking, baking, and whipped cream on berries. This made the fat count of the raw milk we drank at home below whole milk levels. I did not like the taste of pasteurized milk but drank it anyway.

Allen got his initial taste of pasteurized milk when he started first grade; he thought the school's milk tasted terrible. He had to sit at his desk until he choked it down. Sometimes that took over half of his recess. Allen was relieved the following year when chocolate milk became available. The chocolate flavoring made the milk tolerable for Allen, and he did not have to miss any recess. The chocolate milk option quickly became the universal choice. Soon only one or two students opted for white milk. I always chose chocolate.

We were given "goiter pills," grey tablets having a chalky chocolate taste. In the 1950s it was generally believed people were low on iodine. Low iodine sometimes caused "goiters," a large lump on a person's neck. The pills were meant to supplement that deficiency. Some kids did not like them and hid them in their paste jars. Some kids ate their paste.

We did special projects: Valentine boxes, May baskets and topographical structures with hills, valleys, and rivers, formed with goo we made, then painted for special effects. At our daily recess times, we played on the merry-go-round, teeter totter, hobbyhorse, and monkey bars. There was a short steep hill behind the school. Below it was a big field with a baseball diamond. During gym classes, when the weather was favorable, we chose sides and played softball. We played duck-duck-goose, red rover, Simon says, and drop the handkerchief on the upper playground.

Jump rope was my favorite. I had my own rope. We used long ropes too, where one person on each end twirled and others jumped into the fun. Several classmates jumped at one time counting the number of jumps we could master. Sometimes two long ropes were twirled, overlapping each other. Double ropes, called "double dutch," were the most difficult way to jump for any length of time.

When snow fell, kids went sledding on the hill behind the school. We also played fox and goose in the snow, often making crazy trails beyond the basic circle with a plus sign within it. I liked to shuffle my feet through the snow and create twisted trails and then watch my classmates navigate the slippery paths during the game.

One year some of the older girls built a beautiful snowman with a sculpted face. It was the best snowman I ever saw. Later that day our teacher asked us to step over to the south window of our classroom where the view overlooked the playground. We expected a big treat, "maybe a second snowman." The sight was appalling. The snowman had been crashed into a frozen white pile. The teachers addressed the sad situation before any one of us found the distressed snowman on our own. I never heard that anyone got in trouble because of the snowman incident, but it was a sad day for the entire school.

Special events were held in the big auditorium on the second level. The room had a stage and floor space large enough to accommodate school-wide or community assemblies to watch educational films, the annual spelling bee, eighth grade graduation and the like.

The whole school took part in the Christmas program that included contemporary and religious songs and carols. Each student received a bag of candy and an apple at the end of the performance, handed out by Santa Claus. There were occasional special events, too. One time I was in a skit about baseball. I got nervous on stage and messed up my lines, resulting in one of the funniest parts in the middle of the skit being missed. I felt bad because I could not go back and correct my error.

We could not chew gum in the building, nor were we allowed to talk in school unless called on by the teacher. Students that whispered or passed notes got in trouble and could be sent to the principal's office or receive a detention, which consisted of staying after school for 15 or 20 minutes. During class time we could communicate with the teacher by raising our hands for permission. We were given codes for special needs. One finger meant we needed to use the bathroom. Two fingers indicated we wanted to use the library. Three fingers meant we wanted to ask a classmate about an assignment. We could not exploit the three-finger request without the teacher catching on we were abusing it.

Restrooms were in the basement. The only way to access the restrooms was to descend the central staircase to the gray painted cement floor. The boys restroom was to the left, the girls to the right. I did not like being in the restroom alone because there were no windows, and distant furnace rumblings drifted through the walls. It was a friendly social place during recess when classmates were there.

The furnace room was also in the basement. We occasionally watched Augie, the janitor, shovel coal into the huge furnace. Then we'd go outside and breathe in the soot coming out of the chimney.

Double swinging doors at the landing between the first floor and the basement were the entrance into the gymnasium. The gymnasium was directly below the auditorium and had a basketball court with a couple levels of bleachers on the east side. The floor in the gym always had a glossy shine. We could wear only gym shoes that had not been worn outside when we walked on that floor. Occasionally we got to watch a special event or a game played by older students. We did not wear our gym shoes for those events. Rather, we followed our teacher and marched behind her across the edge of the floor by the south wall beneath the basketball hoop to sit on the bleachers.

Some classmates from the village went home to eat lunch, but many stayed at school. I scurried from my classroom and grabbed the brown paper lunch bag, reused from day to day until it ripped and I was rewarded a new one. Dad bought a bushel basket of items at an auction one day, and in the basket were three blue metal lunch boxes with thermoses in the lid that had belonged to the Kowalke family. One had the name Janet inscribed; the others were Gary's and

Bonnie's. We used those lunch boxes on occasion, but we usually carried brown paper bags to school.

When there was a sandwich in the bag, it was cheese and jelly or sausage from our farm. Mom often packed wide mouth thermos containers with soup, leftover casserole or meat, potatoes, and vegetables. We wolfed down our food because we could go to the playground when we finished eating.

I noticed many classmates ate peanut butter sandwiches. They gobbled their sandwich in no time and were usually first on the playground. We did not eat peanut butter at home because we ate what came from our farm. A peanut butter sandwich sounded quite sophisticated to me. After soliciting David and Allen to my side, we approached Mom as a group to persuade her to make peanut butter sandwiches for our lunch. Mom finally gave in; she was probably sick of our whining.

I was already anticipating extra playground time as I grabbed my lunch bag, but by the second mouthful I realized a peanut butter sandwich wrapped in wax paper, sitting in a bag all morning was not that great. I struggled to swallow each bite with gulps of milk, but the foreign peanut butter stuck to the roof of my mouth and in my throat. I had no extra time to play outside that day. The hardest part was telling Mom I did not like peanut butter sandwiches.

Top: Second and third grade students from North Freedom Grade School are enjoying an annual class trip to a bakery followed by riding the 400 Train to Elroy and back. Carolyn is second from the left in the middle row. *Bottom*: The Schroeder children are dressed as a family for the May Day Play Day parade in 1955 and are standing in front of the North Freedom Grade School as the parade ended. Carolyn is dressed as the father, David the mother; Allen is in the buggy.

60

Class Trips and May Day Play Day

The end of the school year had many great events. Class trips were an annual highlight. One year, our class visited Truax Field and the air guard base in Madison where we boarded an airplane and saw the cockpit and control panel. We never got off the ground. Other years, we went to a museum of natural history, Henry Vilas Park and Zoo, Gardner Bakery, the State Capitol, a dairy and rode the 400 train to Elroy. These exotic destinations were places I was sure I would never again see in my lifetime.

Class trips took place in the spring toward the end of the school year. The trip to the museum of natural history was unexpectedly memorable. We arrived at the museum mid-morning. After a welcoming speech, we slowly followed the docent, observing artifacts and listening to history. Eventually, we found ourselves deep in the building in a dimly lighted room surrounded by skeletons and skulls. I shifted from side to side as my stomach started to growl. This was not because of the museum. I was hungry.

It was at this same time there was some rustling within our group. One classmate was laying on the floor. My best friend, Carolyn Myers, told me later, "That's the only time I ever fainted."

She explained the morning was cool, so her mother bundled her into layers of warm clothes. Sunshine had warmed the day nicely by the time we arrived at the museum. Carolyn had no choice but to stay bundled. Additionally, our teachers and chaperones discouraged us from drinking water, for the obvious reason. These conditions, combined with the dimly lit room, packed full of children, and being surrounded with skulls and such, overwhelmed Carolyn.

After moving her into fresh air, placing cool cloths on her head, and giving her a drink of water, Carolyn was fine.

May Day Play Day was an annual event in May. It started with a big parade uptown. We decorated our bicycles with crepe paper woven through the wheel spokes and streamers off the handlebars. Playing cards were tucked into fender bars to make a clacking noise against the spokes as we rolled along. Some children dressed in silly old clothes and hats.

When I was seven, Mom had an idea. She decorated the woven reed baby buggy. I was dressed like a man in some of Dad's old clothes: a hat with earflaps, a necktie, and a taped-on mustache of corn silk that started to unstick by the end of the parade. David was dressed like a woman, including lipstick and one of Mom's little hats. Allen was plunked into the buggy with a baby bonnet and a blanket. My brothers and I were not as thrilled with our costumes as Mom was.

When the parade ended, there was a huge party on the big field behind the school with organized games and races with prizes. Kids sat on the steep hill to watch the events while waiting their turn to participate. My favorite was the three-legged race where one of my legs was tied to someone else's leg and we had to race against other tied together students.

61
Eighth Grade Graduation

Eighth grade graduation was a big deal in 1961. There were 15 students in my class. We were the first of the baby boomers. The four girls wore short formal dresses, and the boys all wore suits and ties for the ceremony. Graduation was held in the auditorium. Our guest speaker was Harland Hill, an attorney from Baraboo. The following year, Harland Hill was appointed a Sauk county judge by former Governor Gaylord Nelson. The stage was decorated with bouquets of fresh flowers from our gardens. Each of us walked across to the podium to receive a diploma from our teacher, Harold Pickar, who was also the principal.

The class banquet followed commencement. Our mothers prepared a delicious meal served to us in the gymnasium by the previous graduating class at a formally set table.

My brother, David, graduated the following year. His was the last eighth grade class to graduate from North Freedom Grade School. The North Freedom School District dissolved and was consolidated with the Baraboo Unified School District in 1961. After that, all seventh and eighth grade students from North Freedom attended Baraboo Junior High School.

In 1991 our grade school building was made into an apartment complex. This was after the new grade school was built north of the cemetery. The old brick school building burned in 2012. There were no injuries, but the building was a total loss. The school building may be gone, but the memories, the village that surrounds the site, and the people who lived there, all helped shape who I am. I feel them in the very core of my being.

Grade school was an intimate experience in North Freedom during the 1950s. Nine of the fifteen classmates graduating with me had started first grade together. Two more joined us by third grade. Three-fourths of the class had spent most of our elementary school years together. I not only knew all of my classmates' names, I knew their parents' names. I knew the color of their eyes. I would turn fourteen years old the weekend after eighth grade graduation and felt prepared to step into my future. Little did I know, expect, or dream of what was ahead of me.

Top: The Eighth Grade Graduation Banquet at the North Freedom Grade School in 1961 was served at a formally set table in the gymnasium. The graduates' mothers prepared the meal and the previous graduating class served. *Bottom*: North Freedom school graduation, Class of 1961. Carolyn is third from the left in the front row.

Acknowledgments

Writing was not on my mind when my brothers and I did farm chores and played in the hayloft. It was not on my mind while raising our daughters or during my professional career. The thought of writing a memoir slammed through me in 2015. To everyone who encouraged me to write and publish my stories, I am eternally grateful. Without encouragement, this book would not have happened. The list is too long to recognize everyone, but I thank each of you from the bottom of my heart.

My brothers David, Allen, and Randy were instrumental in shaping my stories. We experienced the same activities and events, yet each of us was affected differently. Their recollection of machinery, logistics, and people living in the village authenticated my memories. Randy continues to live in North Freedom. I was fortunate to have conversations with him and David. David passed away in January 2020 from gioblastoma.

My brother Allen, mentor and confidant, read my original work, a jumbled mess of thoughts. He continued to reread revised drafts to the end. His recall of situations and conversations were like little gold nuggets that prodded dialog while incorporating history. His impeccable research in tracing land transfers, recalling relatives from past generations, and the ability to remember people living in North Freedom during the 1950s and before, lends credibility to my stories. I am forever grateful for his time, and especially for his encouragement.

There are people whose help went far beyond anything I expected or could have anticipated. Six readers slogged through the unedited manuscript and offered invaluable professional comments. Thank you to Carolyn Myers Blum, Beth and Ken Campshure, Carol Fleishauer, Keri Olson, and Marc Seals. You made my writing better. Special mention goes to my grandson and junior reader, Cooper Herbes.

Carolyn (Myers) Blum read new text, and reread revisions, to the end. Her editing expertise and attention to detail is unmatched. Carolyn's memories of living in the village provided wonderful snippets that enhanced my stories.

I am indebted to the entire team at Cornerstone Press for guiding me through the publication process to make my book a reality. The following people are especially recognized: Gavrielle McClung, senior editorial assistant and my primary editor. Amanda Leibham, cover designer; Jeff Snowbarger, executive editor; Lexie Neeley and Monica Swinick, senior editors; and the entire press staff: Megan Bittner, Kala Buttke, Grace Dahl, Camilla Freund, Kyra Goedken, Brett Hill, Seth Kundinger, Dylan Potter, Cassie Ress, Annika Rice, Abbi Rohde, and Bethany Webb. I owe a special thank you to Dr. Ross Tangedal, the director and publisher, for his confidence in me and for acquiring my manuscript.

I am indebted to Maggie Marquardt, director of development and university advancement for the College of Fine Art and Communication at the University of Wisconsin-Stevens Point, for coordinating my meeting with Dr. Tangedal and Cornerstone Press, a gem that shines at the university.

To everyone who lived in the village of North Freedom during my childhood, you influenced my life for the better. To the many who shared information and memories, your information expanded and authenticated my work.

My talented daughter, Kyla Herbes, built my website. I was lost without her help.

I want to recognize my parents, Harold and Pearl (Kaun) Schroeder, to whom my book is dedicated. Thank you for being the example, and for supporting me even when we did not always agree. You taught me to do, and be, my best. I am grateful for your sense of humor and continue to rely on the wisdom and common sense you instilled in me. I only wish you were here to read my stories.

My memories would not have become a book without the patient understanding of my loving husband of over 55 years. Thank you, David Dallmann, for your support, for reading and rereading, and especially for listening and always being there. To my late daughter Kassi, loved and remembered by many, you should be acting, directing, and writing books of your own. You add dimension to my world because your presence is always with me, in the best way. Thank you to my daughter, Kyla, son-in-law, Thorsten, and grandchildren, Cooper and Zoe, for keeping me grounded; you have heard my stories many times over. You all are the lights of my life!

Bibliography

Blum, Carolyn Myers. *North Freedom School, Elementary Schools and Classmates, The Memory Book*. Baraboo, WI: Baraboo Senior High School, 2015.

Curry, Ross M. *Hidden History of the Wisconsin Dells Area*. The History Press, 2010.

Davies, George. *The Story of the Town of Freedom and Village of North Freedom*, as compiled by a Group of Interested Citizens Who Desire to Preserve the Early memories Handed Down by the Forefathers, Printed by Sauk County Publishing Co., Baraboo Wisconsin. Committee: George Davies, Frank Hanley, Albert Templin, Rose Griep, Henry Griep, Ernest Ristau, Edith Hengstler, Jake Hackett, Laura Bonnell, Minnie Voss; Prepared for the Wisconsin Centennial, 1948.

Dynes, Erica. "Flood-damaged Rocks Springs Community Center to be demolished." *Reedsburg Times-Press*, 2 April 2019. https://www.wiscnews.com/reedsburgtimespress/news/local/flood-damaged-rocks-springs-community-center-to-be-demolished/article_1cf1a745-f615-5bf9-976a-0772818724df.html. Accessed on 28 September 2020.

Good Old Golden Rule Days, Rural Schools Research Committee, Baraboo WI: Sauk County Historical Society, 1994.

"Gopher Bounty Resolution 01-11." Polk County, Wisconsin. January 2011. www.co.polk.wi.us/vertical/Sites/%7BA1D2EAAA-7A29-46D6-BF1A-12B71F23A6E1%7D/uploads/Res2011_01-11_Gopher_Bounty.pdf. Accessed on May 30, 2021.

Mueller, Erhart A. *Only in Sumpter*. Stevens Point, WI: Worzalla Publishing Co., 1977.

"North Freedom, Wisconsin." *City-data.com*. www.city-data.com/city/North-Freedom-Wisconsin.html. Accessed 29 March 2020.

"Oak Hill Cemetery (North Freedom Cemetery)." *Internment.net*. www.interment.net/data/us/wi/sauk/oakhill_nf/index.htm. Accessed 25 July 2018. at:

"Policy 201301." Town of Sheridan, Dunn Count, Wisconsin. https://sheridantownship.org/wp-content/uploads/2015/10/Policy.2013.01.BountyPocketGophers.pdf. Accessed on 30 May 2021.

"Milestones In Railroad History, Famed '400s' Retire; So Do Veteran Conductor, Engineer," *The Capital Times*, Tuesday, 23 July 1963.

"Queen for a Day," *Monrovia Daily*, 17 February 1953.

"Rock Springs – Ableman." Sauk County Historical Society, *Saukcountyhistory.org*. https://saukcountyhistory.org/rock-springs-ableman. Accessed 12 July 2019.

Schroeder, Allen K. *The Old Hackett's Homestead, Where North Freedom, Wisconsin Began*, 2019.

---. *An Overview of North Freedom, Wisconsin Churches, 1847-1900, including Township Churches Close to North Freedom*, 2019.

Schroeder, Todd Alan. *The Schroeder Family Tree*, August 5, 1993.

They Led Us to Today, A History of North Freedom, Wisconsin, Volume 1. Edited by Michael J. Carignan. North Freedom, WI: The Village Board of North Freedom, 2018.

They Led Us to Today, A History of North Freedom, Wisconsin, Volume 2. Edited by Michael J. Carignan. North Freedom, WI: The Village Board of North Freedom, 2000.

Ward, Joseph Wayne. *North Freedom, The First 100 Years*. Grimm Bindery, 2009.

Notes

1. The author gratefully acknowledges the assistance of the following individuals for granting interviews and conversations crucial to the completion of this book: Allen Schroeder, David Schroeder, Randy Schroeder, Carolyn (Myers) Blum, Terri Thomas, Dianne Woelfl Mueller, Victor and Frosteen Beckman, Eber Janzen, Shari (Baumgarten) Luther, Rollie Waddell, Sandy (Fuller) Nehring, Donald "Pete" Leece, Raymond Sorenson, Beverly Vertein, and John Myers.

2. The author wishes to thank the following for granting permission to use particular photographs reproduced in this book: Carolyn (Myers) Blum, Louise Vater Crisman, and the Sauk County Historical Society.

3. Disclaimers:

   a. Oak Hill Cemetery records indicate Dan Seeley died in 1943. However, the author remembers seeing Dan inside their home through the screen door as she talked with Mary when she was a child. Allen Schroeder also remembers when Dan died.

   b. Confirmation of the septic being under the empty lot uptown was not possible. The statement is included in the text because it cannot be disproven and has been repeated over the years by others from the village.

CAROLYN DALLMANN grew up on a family farm within the village limits of North Freedom, Wisconsin. Prior to writing fulltime she worked at the Badger Army Ammunition Plant in Sauk County, Wisconsin, for over thirty years. Her life writing has appeared in the *Wisconsin Magazine of History*, and **North Freedom** is her debut book. Learn more about Carolyn at carolyndallmann.com.

www.ingramcontent.com/pod-product-compliance
Lightning Source LLC
Chambersburg PA
CBHW020132130526
44590CB00040B/378